Challenging Western Christians and Their Neighbours

Challenging Western Christians and Their Neighbours

Be Participants in the Mission of Jesus, At Home and Abroad

Steven Paas

RESOURCE *Publications* · Eugene, Oregon

CHALLENGING WESTERN CHRISTIANS AND THEIR NEIGHBOURS
Be Participants in the Mission of Jesus, At Home and Abroad

Resource Publications
An Imprint of Wipf and Stock Publishers
199 W. 8th Ave., Suite 3
Eugene, OR 97401

www.wipfandstock.com

PAPERBACK ISBN: 978-1-7252-7584-3
HARDCOVER ISBN: 978-1-7252-7573-7
EBOOK ISBN: 978-1-7252-7580-5

Manufactured in the U.S.A.

Layout: Wim Paas

Table of Content

Preface

I have dedicated this booklet to my grandfather, Willem Klein (1887-1959). He was a peat digger in Klazienaveen (Province of Drenthe, The Netherlands). He was physically not strong enough for that heavy work. But after going bankrupt as a peatery owner in the economic crisis of the 1920s, he had no choice. A life of poverty and worries ensued. Grief struck him very deeply when bullets from the German *Sicherheitsdienst* (SD) ended the life of his son in 1944. Through it all, he remained a Christian, as an elder in the local Reformed Church, in his family, and in his relationship with others. In my memory lives the image of a bent little man with a calm face and friendly eyes.

But he's much more to me. I was perhaps about 8 years old, when he squeezed my hand during a walk and said, 'Jesus is the most important thing in your life. He always wants to be with you.' Years later, I realized that these words are a (free) quote of the promise Jesus made following the great commission to His disciples: 'And surely I am with you always, to the very end of the age' (Mt.28:20). I am now well past the age my grandfather was allowed to reach. It moves me that all these years God has used the memory of my grandfather's statement of faith to keep me, especially in times of crisis and darkness. For me, the words of William Klein are still a powerful missionary testimony, which I like to share with the readers of this writing.

The first aim of this booklet is alerting Western Christians, including myself. Soldiers are sometimes sent on mission. A comparison with Christians seems to be obvious, because they are also on mission. But that comparison is faulty. The mission of Christians lasts for the whole of their lives and it begins next door. The status of the Sender of Christians is also different from a military commander. He is Christ. He preceded them, let them participate in His mission, and He is always with them. Unlike the military practice, the working methods of Christians are not offensive or aggressive. As participants in Christ's mission, they serve the people in their context as 'pilgrims and priests'.[1]

I hope that many non-Christians will also be among the readers. For two reasons. They can use the content to determine the effect Christians would like to have on them. It's always good to know what drives someone. The book can also help them to check whether the Christians they know correspond to their intended identity, or whether they may appear not to be true Christians. Also good to know, especially when you feel urged to challenge them with questions.

These words I write in the spring of 2020, when the worldwide corona crisis is reminding the whole of humanity of its vulnerability and dependency. This challenges the proud Western assumption that we are able to make or control our own existence. The lesson for Western Christians and their neighbours is to draw nearer to one another and to God.

I thank my brother Wim Paas for the layout of this writing. I also thank Kees van der Ziel (MA), a former Bible translator in Surinam, and Erik Merx, a supporter of missions, for their corrections and useful advices. Dr.Mark Thiesen has read the manuscript from his experience as a fellow-missionary worker in Malawi and as a pastor in an American setting. His valuable remarks I have gratefully used.

Veenendaal, Spring 2020,

Steven Paas sr.

---

[1] The term I have derived from a book by my son and namesake Stefan [Steven] Paas, by whom/ by which I have been inspired: *Pilgrims and Priests: Christian Mission in a Post-Christian Society*, London: SCM Press, 2019. See also his: *Church Planting in the Secular West: Learning from the European Experience*, Grand Rapids: Eerdmans, 2016.

1. Words from the Sent Lord

a. The Father sends

The words which Jesus used for sending His disciples are sometimes called the 'great commission'. The instruction 'go' in *Matthew* 28 and *Mark* 16 is the meaningful beginning of it. Apparently, Christ has given to His flock on earth – generally named *congregation* or *church* – a missionary task as first priority.

In principle, I do not distinguish between the two terms. They are different sides of the same coin. The word *church* (*kuriakè* = of the Lord) emphasizes that Christ is her Lord (*kurios*) or Head. Here, I often use the name *congregation*, because it emphasizes that the Body of Christ[2] is a universal community of members belonging together, and at the same time a local form of it that can be observed by anyone in the neighbourhood.

That missionary task has been entrusted to us as Christians. Do we – individually and as a congregation – still participate in it wholeheartedly? The mission of Christians is a high calling, for it does not stand alone. It has been derived from the task Jesus Christ has received. God the Father sent His Son to the world! He himself is and remains the Sent One, who precedes us. After His ascension, the mission of the Son has continued through the spread of the gospel and the work of the Holy Spirit. The fact that Christians have a mission, therefore, means that they have been included in the mission of God the Son by God the Father.

That starting point is referred to as the *Missio Dei*, the Mission of God. Christopher Wright says the whole Bible stems from God's mission and deals with God's mission, with the aim of claiming back the fallen world for His Kingdom. In the Bible, God lays the foundation for His all-embracing ('holistic') mission in the world and for the role Christians have to

---

[2] Rom.12:5; 1 Cor.12:12-27; Eph.3:6; 4:15,16; 5:23; Coll.1:18,24.

9

play in it.[3] Mission is the work of God, from beginning to end. It is God's mission, not the mission of us as Christians or of the church.

Our missionary activities are not so much answering to the mission of Jesus, but rather they are participating in the mission of God. Bauckham shows how God in the Biblical record of His mission in the world always calls a certain individual to make Himself known to all people in the context of that person. Every individual Christian is such a missionary for his or her surroundings. God makes him or her a missionary in and through Jesus Christ.[4] *Acts* 8:4 shows that as Christians fled the Jerusalem persecution after the ascension of Jesus they became missionaries wherever they went.

Apart from calling of all Christians to mission, Gods has gifted a number of Christians to be missionaries in a special manner. Long before, the prophets of the Old Testament have reported how through specifically called persons God began to pave the way for His Son (Is. 40:3; Mal.3:1;cf. Mk.1:2.3). The evangelist John explains *why* God paved the way for the arrival of His Son. The reason He sent Christ is His love for the world.

> 'For God so loved the world that He gave His one and only Son, that whoever believes in Him shall not perish but have eternal life' (John 3:16).

> 'This is how God showed His love among us: He sent His one and only Son into the world that we might live through Him' (1 Joh.4:9).

The love of God the Father for the world means that He loves the people. He does not want to condemn people so that they die. He wants to save people. He desires all to be saved (John 3:17; 1 Tim.2:3,4). That is why He sent Jesus, His Son. God the Son has carried that love into the world. He is God's love. Jesus

---

[3] Christopher J.H. Wright, *The Mission of God: Unlocking the Bible's Grand Narrative*, InterVarsity, 2013.

[4] Richard Bauckham, *The Bible and Mission: Christian Witness in a Postmodern World*, Baker Publ., 2004.

has not only come to save the souls of men. The Father has commissioned Him to save the whole of man, soul and body, that is, *all* of *all* who believe in Him.

> 'All that the Father gives Me will come to Me, and whoever comes to Me I will never drive away. For I have come down from heaven not to do My will but to do the will of Him who sent Me. And this is the will of Him who sent Me, that I shall lose none of all that He has given Me, but raise them up at the last day. For My Father's will is that everyone who looks to the Son and believes in Him shall have eternal life, and I will raise him up at the last day' (John.6:37-40).

As early as at the beginning of His sojourn on earth, Jesus pointed to His special task, when He quoted the prophet Isaiah:

> 'The Spirit of the Lord is on Me, because He has anointed Me to preach good news to the poor. He has sent Me to proclaim freedom for the prisoners and recovery of sight for the blind, to release the oppressed, to proclaim the year of the Lord's favour' (Lk. 4:18,19; cf. Is. 61:1,2).

Humans are the crown of creation. The fact that Jesus saves people means that He is going to save all creation. God loves His whole creation. Therefore, a new beginning has been made in Christ, so that God will achieve His universal purpose for creation. There will be a new heaven and a new earth (Rev.21:1).

Jesus Christ is the greatest love gift God has given to the world, to humanity. Unbelievers and ignorant people do not recognize this gift. Therefore, they are in the dark, trapped in the dangerous situation of death and sin. But believers recognize this gift. They know Christ. That is the very characteristic of faith. Believers extend their hands to this gift of God the Father. They accept Christ and embrace Him as their Saviour.

But faith pertains to more than that. Believers not only agree that Christ has been sent to the world, but they also accept that they themselves have been sent by Him. We see that this full acceptance of Christ was reflected by the relationship between Jesus and His first disciples. The love He received from His Father Jesus wants to carry into the world through His disciples.

b. The Son sends

The apostles, i.e. the first disciples of Jesus, followed His example as the One who had been sent. In turn, they were sent by Him. They were meant to be sent. This is evidenced first of all by the revealed communication between God the Father and God the Son.

> Jesus said to the Father: 'As You sent Me into the world, I have sent them into the world' (John 17:18).

The fact that the apostles were sent is also evident in what Jesus Himself said to them:

> 'And this gospel of the kingdom will be preached in the whole world as a testimony to all nations, and then the end will come' (Mt.24:14).

> 'Then Jesus came to them and said: All authority in heaven and on earth has been given to Me. Therefore go and make disciples of all nations, baptising them in the name of the Father and of the Son and of the Holy Spirit and teaching them to obey everything I have commanded you. And surely I am with you always, to the very end of the age' (Mt.28:18-20).

> 'He said to them: Go into all the world and preach the good news to all creation. Whoever believes and is baptised will be saved, but whoever does not believe will be condemned' (Mk. 16:15,16).

> 'Then He opened their minds so they could understand the Scriptures. He told them: This is wat is written: The Christ will suffer and rise from the dead on the third day, and repentance and forgiveness of sins will be preached in His name to all nations, beginning at Jerusalem'' (Lk. 24:45-47).

The status of the being-sent of Jesus and of the first disciples is referred to as the apostolate, a word derived from the Greek verb *apostello*: sending. The verb radiates urgency. Jesus Himself was the first One who was sent. Therefore, in *Hebrews* 3:1 He is called Apostle. He handed over the apostleship to His first disciples, the apostles. In turn, the apostles have transferred the status of being-sent to their successors. As Jesus was sent by God the Father and as He himself sent His first disciples, so He sends all those who believe in Him into the world. Not as chasers after fame and power, but as 'servants' (1 Cor.4:1) 'foot washers' (John.13). Christ Himself gave an example to all His followers. In the 'apostolic succession', He lays His blessing hands on all Christians.

He sends all believers to testify to the great love God gave to them, and to pass it on. Jesus Himself is that love gift. He sends them to testify to Himself. After His resurrection from the grave, He appeared to His first disciples with the mission to spread in words and deeds the good news of deliverance, reconciliation, peace and renewal. This mission the first disciples have passed on to their successors, ultimately to all believers. Regardless of their origin and background, all believers have received a mission from God. He has sent us into the world to make a difference; not to be passive observers, but to be dedicated vicars of Him in all situations, however dangerous, in order to attract people to Jesus and work for His peace and justice. He sent us to feed the hungry, to give water to the thirsty, to dress the nude, to give freedom to prisoners, to take care of people who are deadly ill and of the orphans and widows. They also oppose war, violence, oppression and injustice, with the prospect of *Isaiah* 2:2-5, that according to God's will, the nations once 'will beat their swords into ploughshares and their spears into pruning hooks'.

In short, believing men and women are called to tell the world in which they live that God is loving and merciful and that He gives deliverance from sin and death to all who in faith surrender to Christ. He is the Prince of Peace, the Good Shepherd who has said of His sheep: 'I have come that they may have life, and have it to the full' (John 10:10b). Christ promises peace and rest to weary and burdened people (Mt.11:28). He has gauged the depth of their suffering because of sin, guilt, diseases and death. And if they are not yet aware of their emergency situation, He wants them to discover it. Not to leave them in it, but to tell them the good news that in Him there is redemption. Spreading that good news is an assignment to all believers. They are the mouth and hands of Christ in His global mission of love.

c. The Holy Spirit sends

But isn't that too much to require from us? Are believers able to carry out that enormous mission? After all, in all aspects of their personal lives they are occupied with the battle against the works of Satan. They are also hindered by the hostile world and their own limitations, weaknesses, and remaining sins. However, God has taken that reality into account. We already noted that not only God the Father and God the Son are involved in the mission task of the disciples. The work of the Holy Spirit, the third Person of the Divine Trinity, is also indispensable.

> 'Again Jesus said: Peace be with you! As the Father has sent Me, I am sending you. And with that He breathed on them, and said: Receive the Holy Spirit' (John 20: 21,22).

> 'He [Jesus] said to them …: But you will receive power when the Holy Spirit comes on you, and you will be My witnesses in Jerusalem, and in all Judea and Samaria, and to the ends of the earth' (Acts 1:7,8).

The Holy Spirit is the One who makes the Word of God to be understood and He leads people to Jesus. The Feast of Pentecost in *Acts* 2 is a wonderful demonstration of the work of the Holy Spirit that breaks through in the world. First of all, the Holy Spirit showed believers that they need salvation, but then He also gives the strength and wisdom to persevere in faith and spread it in the world. He enables them to do so, by giving to every believer his or her own gifts (1 Cor.12-14).

The involvement of the Father, the Son and the Holy Spirit shows the trinitarian character of the apostolate, in particular of the 'great commission'. In *Matthew* 28, Jesus even mentions the three Persons in one verse (:19). The same tri-une God who loves, saves and renews lost people is behind it. This emphasises the importance and urgency of the missionary character of Christians, individually and together in the context of the congregation.

The position of being-sent in the world of Christians cannot be taken for granted by them. The characteristic of a Christian is that he or she participates in the One who has been sent, Jesus Christ. Christians are part of the great mission of Christ. The love of Him urges them to comply with it (2 Cor.5:14). In all their weakness and sometimes doubts, they worship Him (Mt.28:17) and obediently receive His missional words.

15

2. The Identity of the Sent Lord

a. The Creator and Re-creator

When Jesus Christ, at the end of His life on earth, according to the Gospels and Acts, passes His mission to the disciples, He includes the church of all times and places, that is all in world history who belong to Him in faith.

In His great commission the Lord first comes to us as God the Son, who is the Creator of heaven and earth. After all, John says that He is the Word, which was not only from the beginning with God, but also was God (John 1:1). John continues in verse 3: 'Through Him all things were made, without Him nothing was made that has been made'. This means two things: (1) Christ was there before He was born as the man Jesus; He was there even before creation took place; (2) The work of Christ concerns all creation, it is of universal significance to all mankind. Paul confirms the cosmic dimension of Christ when he describes Him as follows in *Colossians* 1:15-17:

> 'He is the image of the invisible God, the firstborn over all creation. For by Him all things were created: things in heaven and on earth, visible and invisible, whether thrones or powers or rulers, or authorities; all things were created by Him. He is before all things, and in Him all things hold together'.

In His mission assignment, we also meet Jesus as the Re-creator. He did not abandon His creation when it lost its perfection through man's sinful disobedience to God and got ruined by the subsequent invasion of death. Then Christ intervened as the all-embracing powerful ruler of His entire creation. Facing Satan and man's fall into sin, He acted in the capacity of the Re-creator, who aimed at the restoration of all things. For that matter, already before creation He had declared Himself willing to take on that task (Ps. 40:8; Hebr.10:7). The tri-une God did not acquiesce in the lost state of man and world. That is why He made his covenant of grace with humanity. As the God of the covenant (YHWH), Christ became the embodiment of that universal covenant of grace throughout the Old Testament. It began when God gave in *Genesis* 3:15 the mother of all promises to Adam and Eve. and it then continued in His acts with believers like Abel, Seth, Enoch, Noah, Melchizedek, Abraham, Isaac, Jacob, and Israel. God's unique relationship with the chosen people of Israel does not mean that He lost sight of the world. His acts with Israel serve as a demonstration to the world of His grace and judgment. In the histories, poetry and prophecies of the Old Testament, God the Son comes to Israel as the angel of the covenant, as the Descendant ('Seed') and Son of Abraham, as Son of David and as the Messiah. But as the Son of Adam and Noah, He also comes to all mankind in the same capacity. His origin from Abraham and His origin from Adam are evident from the pedigree of Jesus in *Matthew* 1:1-16 and *Luke* 3:23-38.[5]

He is the Saviour, the Re-creator, first as a foreshadowing in the prophecies to Israel. But intertwined with that, the Messiah – made concrete in Jesus i.e. in His humiliation and exaltation – is the Re-creator for the whole world. The writer of the epistle to the *Hebrews* shows that concisely:

'In the past God spoke to our forefathers through the prophets at many times, and in various ways, but in these days He has spoken to us by His Son, Whom He appointed heir of all things, and through Whom He made the universe. The Son is the radiance of God's glory and the exact representation of His being, sustaining all things by His powerful Word. After He had provided purification of sins, He sat down at the right hand of the Majesty in heaven.

---

[5] The Reformer John Calvin explained the difference between these two pericopes: In the list of Matthew, Christ seems to be destined only for the descendants of Abraham. But when Jesus Christ is called [by Luke] Son of Noah and Son of Adam, we see that His grace extends to everywhere. And although we do not belong to that holy lineage that God once had chosen and accepted, yet our Lord Jesus has been given to us. Because we need a saving resource as well as they do. Well, this tool of salvation is generally valid, and for all. That is the cause of the distinction between what we find here in the story of *Matthew* and *Luke*. [Translated from: *Het gepredikte Woord: Preken van Johannes Calvijn*, vert. door J. Douma en W. H. van der Vegt, Franeker: T. Wever 1978 (via RD, 28-12-19)].

So He became as much superior to the angels as the name He has inherited is superior to theirs' (Hebr.1:1-4).

b. Son of David

The universal significance of Jesus Christ the Son of God for all mankind does not contradict His Jewish identity and His significance as 'Son of David'. The Son of God was born as scion of the Jewish remnant of the people of Israel. Through His mother Mary, He was a Jew in terms of ethnicity. Through His foster father Joseph, He was connected to the family line of King David (Mt.1:1; cf. Lk.1:32). That is why, in the expectation of many Jews He was the Messiah King, who would restore the empire of David. The Roman occupiers realized this sentiment. The humiliating cross on which they executed Him had a ridiculing inscription: 'the King of the Jews'.

Today, many Christians are interested in a revaluation of the Jewish roots of Christianity and the Jewish identity of Jesus. In regards to this interest it is important to keep in mind that the gospel is equally valid for both the Jews and the Gentiles.[6] This is often not well understood, especially if a connection is made to Jewish religious and cultural views and writings that have no place for Jesus as the Son of God and Messiah.[7] Nevertheless, acknowledging that Jesus was a Jew in His being connected to Abraham and to the second king of Israel, is of great importance, for at least two reasons:

First, the Jewish ethnic identity of Jesus emphasizes that He was a true man of flesh and blood. Christ did not seemingly appear in a human body, neither did He bring from heaven a glorified, spiritual body, which had only passed through Mary

---

[6] Bosch, *Transforming Mission,* p.92, emphasizes this based on the books of *Luke*: 'Luke wrote his two-volume work for the benefit of Jews as much as Gentiles'.

[7] Cf. Steven Paas, *Israëlvisies in beweging: Gevolgen voor kerk, geloof en theologie*, Kampen: Brevier 2014. Idem, *Christian Zionism Examined: A Review of Ideas on Israel, the Church, and the Kingdom.* Second edition, Eugene, Oregon: Wipf & Stock, 2020.

'like water through a tube', as the Gnostics[8] believe. Such ideas undermine the miracle that – with the exception of sin – He was equal to us in everything and that, as a man – by birth, suffering, dying, descent into hell and resurrection – in our place, He has truly overcome the power of death and sin. If He had not been a real human being, His power as the vicarious victor would be unreliable. Then it would be pointless to praise Him as the Saviour of the world and as our personal Saviour.

Secondly, the Jewish identity of Jesus confirms the credibility and reliability of the Old Testament. In Him, the Old Testament receives its essential meaning for humanity. In the parable of *Matthew* 13:52, about the storeroom of the Word of God, Jesus mentions the new treasures first. In the light of His newness, the old treasures get their actual luster. This applies to the promises made to Adam, Noah and Abraham. It also applies to all aspects of God's acts with the Old Testament people of Israel. In the new form of the covenant of grace Jesus brings Israel to fulfilment and He shows its ultimate meaning. He takes the place of Israel, as it were. The description of this reality is often rejected, under the pretext that it would justify an anti-Jewish replacement theology in which the Church and the Christians would take the place of Israel. However, the Church or the Christians do not replace Israel, but rather the Old Testament Israel comes to its own in Jesus, because He is the long-awaited Messiah.

He is the Son of David. This is not necessarily evident from a DNA relationship with David, but from the fact that He represents the Davidic family lines in *Matthew* 1:1-17 and *Luke* 3:23-38. In that way, King David, together with the generations before and after him, receive their true place in the history of God's revelation, namely by the fact that the Jew Jesus, the Son of David, is the Christ, Who shines His light upon them.

As a result, the Old Testament as a book of Israel is given an essential and surprising fulfilment (cf. 1 Cor.2:8,9;

---

[8] A short but clear description of the phenomenon of Gnosticism can be found in: Jonathan Hill, *Christianity, the First 400 Years*, Lion Hudson, 2013, chapter 7.

Is.53). It also becomes the book of Jesus Christ. Martin Luther points to two aspects of the Old Testament as the 'Book of Christ' (*Buch von Christus*). It leads people to Christ, and at the same time it is full of Him. The Old Testament office of Moses receives its true meaning from Jesus.[9] Some Christians find it difficult to recognize that the Old Testament in all its aspects is about Christ in that it is always pointing people to Him.[10]

Of course it is right to say that the true believers in the Old Testament did not yet know Jesus. But they knew about the coming Christ, in other words the 'Spirit of Prophecy', which testifies to Jesus (Rev.19:10) was in them. Abraham and Moses had a view of Christ (Hebr.11:10, 26,27). They were not the only ones. Although the future was still hidden from them in shadows and symbols, they realized that the Old Testament revelations received their meaning and purpose from the coming Messiah, whose identity gradually took shape in those writings. By the birth of Jesus, the meaning of the shadows and symbols came to light and their full universal significance was shown. This is not recognized at the expense of the Jewish identity of Messiah Jesus and the Jewish character of the Old Testament, but it gives these identities their ultimate meaning. It confirms that the Old Testament remains the Word of God, in which His Son has approached as the Saviour for all inhabitants of the earth of all times and places, who believe in Him.

---

[9] Martin Luther, *Weimarer Ausgabe* 12, S.274, 275. Via: Steven Paas, *Luther on Jews and Judaism: A Review of his 'Judenschriften'*, Zürich: LIT Verlag, 2017, p.11-24

[10] Cf. a study by theologians in one of the Reformed denominations in the Netherlands, about the meaning of the name 'Israel' in church and theology ("Wat betekent de term 'Israël' in kerk en theologie?"). In the introduction, the writers assert without any nuance that the New Testament as well as the Old Testament constitute the Book of Israel (p.1). The rest of the study (on portions of Scripture, history, contemporary debate, consequences) is based on this one-sided theory [file:///C:/Users/Gebruiker/Downloads/9.03-p.1-51-rapport-kerk-en-Israel%20(2).pdf].

c. Darkened Identity

Meanwhile, many have not understood the Jewish Jesus nor the Old Testament from which He rises as Son of God and Messiah. They have darkened Christ's identity by adapting it to their own philosophy or image of God. They include Christians, Jews, and others.

It is generally acknowledged that the *Tanakh*, as the Jews call the Old Testament, is an impressive collection of histories, poetry, wisdom literature and prophecies of venerable antiquity. Virtually, all aspects of life are discussed, attractive aspects (love, mercy, sacrifice, selflessness, fidelity, sincerity, beauty, peace, grace), and ugly aspects (hatred, cruelty, violence, selfishness, war, deceit, lies, destruction, abominations, judgment, death). The content is rich and there is a large difference between genres and subjects. Who can bind that great number of sometimes difficult and opposing categories together into one perspective, which clarifies their purpose?

The answer is to be found in the identity of the Jew Jesus Christ. Having problems with the nature of Christ and misunderstanding the Old Testament go hand in hand. This is what history has shown. Many got stuck in understanding the Old Testament and therefore they failed in seeing who Christ is. Among them were Christians, like Marcion[11] in Antiquity. They considered the descriptions of ethical misdeeds, atrocities, violence and immorality in the Old Testament as bizarre and aimless, and therefore they abolished it as God's revelation, although they often continued to appreciate it as a literary product. Consequently, they mistakenly created an image of Jesus that is only derived from the New Testament. By isolating the New Testament and by misinterpreting and abandoning

---

[11] Peter J. Thomson, 'Harnack, Marcion: das Evangelium vom fremden Gott' [Internet] discusses the influential study by Adolf Harnack (1851-1930) about Marcion, who was declared an heretic by the congregation in Rome in the year 144 AD. Thomson concludes: 'Joining in with the anti-Semitic spirit of the age, he [Harnack] also propagated Marcion's radical rejection of the Old Testament as a recipe for healing twentieth century Christianity'.

the Old Testament as God's revelation, they darkened for themselves and for others the appearance of the true identity of Jesus.

Those Jews, who became followers of the religion and culture of Judaism, more or less applied a reversed order. From the beginning of the New Testament era they have rejected Jesus, not necessarily His existence and identity as a Jew, but His identity as the Son of God and the Messiah. By rejecting the Jew Jesus Christ, the religion of Judaism has demoted the *Tanakh* to a book of religious, nationalist and racial nature, in which the other peoples are defined as second-class.

Perhaps Western culture has nurtured the most widespread form of misunderstanding and abuse of both the true identity of Jesus and the intention of the Old Testament. Western culture is in some ways a product of successful christianisation, but only partially because from its very earliest stages of development the form of Christianity was only nominal. That has been featured in at least two ways. First, the Western empires (starting with the Roman Empire) considered themselves as chosen successors or replacements of Old Testament Israel. Second, many used the name of Christ as a label, without following Him. Christ became a cultural hero. This has led to the mistaken picture of the true nature of both Old Testament Israel and of Christ.

The consequences were serious. In the Western, 'Christian' culture the image of the spiritual Kingdom of Christ characterized by love, peace and justice for all soon faded. Dominant became the pursuit of the core ideals of power, wealth, prosperity, expansion and growth. This happened at the expense of the weakest in the societies and of the most vulnerable aspects of God's creation. An example of cultural derailment is the long, bloody history of Western conquests and violent submissions within Europe, but especially in Asia, Africa and the Americas, which were often motivated by the contention that the representatives of the Western Christian culture, or the 'new Israel', were called by God to do so.

Under the pretext of a divine mandate to spread Christian civilization, crusades and brutal wars, slave trade and slavery[12] were defended, together with colonialism, imperialism, apartheid, genocide,[13] Holocaust, unbridled economic growth, and exploitation of the resources of the earth. One may argue that history has also shown the positively reforming and healing side of (Western) Christianity. Yes, there was slavery, but the move to abolish slavery began among the Christians. Yes, there has been anti-Semitism and even a Holocaust, but also Christians were hiding Jews and saving them when they could. Yes, the colonies were raped by 'Christians', but there were also faithful Christians that tried to stop this. The very idea of human rights came from a Western Christian background. The so-called Christian nations were doing grave injustices, but so were the other nations when they could. The only hope for redeeming any of these peoples, Western or otherwise, is the transformative message of Jesus.

Yet nations and cultures which considered themselves Christian were more responsible, because they could have known better. Western world domination has recently been described by Tom Holland, for example in his book bearing the telling title, *Dominion*. He admits that Christianity, as the 'most influential heritage of the old world', has not only positively

---

[12] An example of ecclesiastical involvement in slavery in North America has been described by Gerald F. DeJong, *The Dutch Reformed Church and Negro Slavery in Colonial America*, reprint from *Church History*, 1971, vol. xxx, No.4.

[13] The most shameful examples of land grabbing and genocide in the name of Christian civilization may be found on both American continents. This is very poignantly, written about by the indigenous Christian author Thomas Michael McDonald, *The Black Book: Native Americans and the Christian Experience – Overcoming the Negative Impact of Nominal Christianity*, Manitoba, Canada: Goldrock Press, 2017 (first, 2004). Cf. Floor van Noortwijk, 'Canada's gebroken mozaiek: Een multiculturele natie verwikkeld in een verleden vol mythes?', BA-thesis, University of Utrecht, 2019.

influenced Western history, but has also proven to be revolutionary and disruptive for many in the world.[14]

To that series of disturbing consequences of Western domination also belongs the seemingly opposing duo of (Western) replacement thinking and (Jewish) Zionism. Both thought systems have appropriated an 'Israel' that does not rest on God's intention with Israel in His Word. Anti-Semitism (hatred of Jews) and philo-Semitism (worshipping Jews) are the extreme consequences. Much of the history of the Jews has developed within Western culture. Often Jews were victims of that culture. The pogroms and the Holocaust are the shameful examples of this.[15] Fortunately, today political and ecclesiastical opinion-makers widely recognize that European culture has been responsible for and guilty of much of the persecution of Jews. There is also a great deal of awareness of the need to suppress the resurgence of anti-Semitism.

But although Jews were often second-class citizens in Western and Eastern Europe, they also participated in cultures that subjected other peoples or put them into slavery.[16] In the attitude of the modern State of Israel towards its Arab inhabitants and the Palestinian territories, we see at least signs of what reminds of those Western examples of oppression and violence. But the Jew Jesus Christ teaches us that the land and the whole

---

[14] Tom Holland, *Dominion: The making of the Western Mind*, Little Rock UK, January 2019..

[15] Many details of 'Christian' involvement in harrassing and persecuting Jews can be found in: J.G.B. (Hans) Jansen, *Christelijke theologie na Auschwitz*, deel 3: *De geschiedenis van 2000 jaar kerkelijk antisemitisme*, Amsterdam: Blaak, 1999.

[16] An example from the Dutch-Surinam history concerns the Jewish planters/ slaveholders, described by e.g. Cynthia McLeod in her story (adapted for the screen): *The Cost of the Sugar,* London: HopeRoad, 2013. Cf. Franklin Steven Jabini, *Christianity in Suriname: An Overview of its History, Theologians and Sources*, Carlisle: Langham, 2012. Jabini indicated that Jews too were involved in the slave trade in Surinam. In 1862, a number of 1394 Jews lived in Surinam (p. 96, 106). He says: 'A large group of the Surinamese elite was Jewish. They looked down on the rest of the population' (p. 114).

earth are of Him. That Biblical message, of which Christ is the centre, crosses out all strategies of conquest and power. For the gospel, all nations are of equal value!

The damage that the black pages of Western culture have caused to Christianity is enormous. The credibility of the proclaimers of the gospel of Christ has become doubtful in the ears of those traditionally exploited, oppressed and deprived of their cultural identity by the West. Also our own Western society, which has been secularized in the meantime, asks probing questions. Why should church leaders, preachers and other Christians be trustworthy and attractive for public opinion if they proclaim the love and grace of Christ, but at the same time condone the unjust relationships in the world or conceal, and overvalue kinship with religions or ideologies in which Christ has no place in principle?[17] Such contradictions are considered hypocritical. They betray an internal weakening of Christianity, thereby undermining Christian testimony towards the world.

d. The Immanuel

In His 'great commission', Jesus approaches us as Creator, Re-creator, God who became man, and as the Jewish Messiah who fulfilled the Scriptures. He also comes to His first disciples and to us as the Immanuel. The Hebrew word means: 'God [is] with us'. The prophet *Isaiah* uses that term in 7:14 and 8:8 to foresay the advent of the Messiah, and in *Matthew* 1:23 that prophetic statement is literally quoted. Jesus applies the name Immanuël to Himself when transferring His mission to the disciples. He says to the them: 'And surely, I am with you always, to the very end of the age' (Mt.28:20). Jesus also applies the promise of His sustaining presence to all the successors to whom the disciples have passed on the mission, for He has added an adjunct of time: 'always, to the very end of the age'. Witnesses of the message of Jesus in words and deeds – and these are basically all true Christians – may count on God to stand by them, for Jesus is 'God with us'.

---

[17] Cf. chapter 4 section d; chapter 5 section c.

But was God 'with us' in our Western culture, when Christianity was cooperating with the powers? In the previous paragraph, we highlighted Western politics of world domination. That phenomenon had an impact on theology. Theological systems were developed on which mission mission strategies were based, which benefited from the violent conquest and subjugation of foreign countries, peoples and cultures. The South-African theologian Kobus van Wyngaard shows that this development in theology is based on the centuries-old idea that the West is the chosen successor to biblical Israel. which in the 19th century connected to the emergence of racist theories. A 'white theology' was born, in which not only the Church had replaced Israel, but which at the same time declared all non-Western cultures and religious ideas inferior. In the colonies of the Western powers, this theory evoked the practice of 'apartheid' between races. In South Africa it became a legal institution.[18]

This explains why the spread of Christianity was not rarely accompanied by the destruction or deprivation of non-Western peoples, customs and languages, without respecting the valuable and beautiful aspects of these cultures. Should we not wonder whether a serious failure to understand the Jew Jesus – Who fulfilled the Old Testament and in Whom God wants to be with us – is a cause of the ecclesiastical malaise and theological confusion within the once 'Christian' culture of the West? And is not the consequence of this evidenced by much inability to participate in Christ's mission?

Our Christianity seems to be trapped in a Western culture that is laden by feelings of guilt and superiority bias. How can that captivity be ended? The Zambian preacher Chopo Mwanza says that Western Christians must first learn that their worldview is not necessarily equal to a Biblical worldview. To

---

[18] George Jacobus (Cobus) van Wyngaard, *In Search of Repair: Critical white responses to whiteness as a theological problem – a South African contribution*, doctoral thesis, Vrije Universiteit, Amsterdam, December 2019, p.45-57. Cf. J. Verkuijl, *Breek de muren af!: Om gerechtigheid in de rassenverhoudingen*, Baarn: Bos & Keuning, 1971.

acknowledge this truth requires a change of attitude and making room for reconnecting to Scripture.[19] The gospel must be liberated from 'the cowboys'. That is what the Christian author Richard Twiss says. He belongs to the original inhabitants of America, who have suffered greatly from the violence of Western culture. For him the 'cowboys' are the representatives of a Christianity that spread violently and without love, with the assumption that the Immanuel was on their side. If Christianity of the West is to regain credibility, basic conversion to Christ is necessary, and theological reorientation to the Sent Lord, who has become their Sender.[20]

---

[19] Chopo Mwanza, 'To Western Missionaries: From an African Pastor' [internet].

[20] Richard Twiss, *Rescuing the Gospel from the Cowboys: A Native American Expression of the Jesus Way*, Downers Grove: Inter Varsity Press 2015 (first, 1996, 2004, 2007).

3. The Sent Lord has become Sender

a. At mission school

When the disciples were sent by Jesus, they had been at the mission school of Jesus for three years. That was the best preparation you can think of. From the beginning of Jesus' public appearance, they had been 'eyewitnesses and servants of the Word' (Lk.1:2). Twice Jesus had sent His disciples for a practical training on the job, to put into practice what they had learnt from Him (Lk.9:1-6; 10:1-20). Then they were not yet able to grasp and spread the depth and breadth of the gospel. For the final work of Jesus in death on the cross, grave and resurrection had not yet taken place.

The concluding part of the missionary teaching by Jesus the disciples received during the 40 days (Acts 1:3) after His resurrection. The teaching ends in the words of the 'great commission' that we quoted in chapter 1. Jesus has overcome death and grave. For that reason, He can now initiate His missionary assignment by saying: 'All authority in heaven and on earth has been given to Me'. Only now Jesus reveals to His disciples the ultimate purpose of His teaching and the function of the tradition of Moses and the Prophets. For,

> 'then He opened their minds so they could understand the Scriptures. He told them: This is what is written: The Christ will suffer and rise from the dead on the third day' (Lk.24:45).

Here Jesus is connecting His own being-sent to the mission of the disciples. He was sent to the world to make reconciliation between God and people. Now the world needs to be informed about His accomplished work. That is why He says to the disciples: 'Peace be with you! As the Father has sent Me, I am sending you' (John 20:21).[21]

---

[21] Lesslie Newbigin, *The Gospel in a Pluralist Society*, Eerdmans, 1989, p.13 - 36.

b. The missionary actions

By His 'great commission' Jesus puts His disciples to work. Their mission consists of six verbs that express action. At the same time they are the various aspects of what Jesus means by mission.

1. *Go*

In *Matthew* 28:19 Jesus says to the disciples: 'Therefore go …'. Mark puts it this way: 'Go into …'. (Mk.16:15). The verb form comes from the Greek *poreúomai*. It means going in the sense of 'going somewhere with something' or 'transporting something to the final destination'. The sent person must move with the gospel one way or another, with a certain purpose. Because the joyful message has a destination, (very) nearby and (sometimes very) far away. The gospel must be *taken* to a place and to persons.

2. *Make disciples*

The verb form used by Jesus in: 'Make disciples of all nations' (Mt.28:19, comes from the Greek verb *mathēteúō* (to educate) and the noun *mathētēs*, which means disciple or pupil. Disciples are true followers of Jesus, through faith and repentance. The first disciples were thus summoned by Him to find people in 'all nations', who are willing to become disciples of Jesus and to follow Him. Increasingly, they learned that activity from Jesus Himself. They grew in knowing and obeying Him. Following Jesus, that must also be learnt by all successive disciples.

For us, the teaching by Jesus is to be found in the Word of God. Learning from the Word is the very characteristic of the ongoing process of discipleship. From children in faith, pupils normally grow into matured believers. During the whole of their lives they receive education in the truths of Scripture and in how to live in accordance with it. They also help others to be disciples of Jesus in daily practice.

3. *Teach*

The activity of 'teaching' in the missional words of Jesus is a special aspect of the concept of 'making disciples' preceding it. Making disciples consists of teaching something to them: 'teaching them to obey everything I have commanded you' (Mt.28:19). The word comes from the Greek verb *didásko*, recognizable in the English word 'didactics'. It means: instructing, communicating knowledge, spreading information. It is a very important and common word in the New Testament and it almost always refers to teaching the Scriptures. The words of Jesus are at the heart of Scripture. Therefore, the content of Scripture is equal to the message that Jesus want us to teach. It is 'everything I have commanded you' (Mt.28:19).

The form of the Greek verb *entéllomai* (to command) makes the instruction of Jesus urgent. It is about 'everything' Jesus has 'commanded' to the disciples. When commanding to carry out His mission, Jesus has in mind a purpose. The disciples and the pupils they recruit must preserve or obey[22] the whole of His teaching, which includes the mission to pass it on.

What does Jesus mean by the whole of His teaching? When at the end of His life on earth He speaks about everything He has commanded, He undoubtedly refers to the content of the Scriptures of the Old Testament. He identifies Himself with these Scriptures. In *Luke* 24 He explained to His fellow travellers to Emmaus what was written concerning Himself 'in all the Scriptures' from *Genesis* to *Malachi* (Lk.24:27). In the Scriptures of the New Testament, He emerged from the Old Testament shadows, as was described by the evangelists and apostles. From the whole of the Bible, the disciples and their successors must pass on to the world who and what Jesus is. He entrusts to them as it were His identity as the Sent One. Like the Father sent Him, He sends them (John 17:18).

He has summed up the nature and content of His commandments in the *Sermon on the Mount* (Mt.5-7). This is the

---

[22] The Greek verb *tēréō,* is used, which means: to preserve, to keep, to guard, to maintain.

constitution of His Kingdom. The core message of Jesus is an articulation of the Father's love for the world (John 3.16). Jesus clarifies the foundation of the Word of God on which the whole content of the Scripture depends. It is His dual commandment of love, as it is described in *Matthew* 22:37-40 and *Mark* 12:30.31. It wants us to love God as the first and highest priority. At the same time it says that we should love our fellow human beings and that we should love them not less than we love ourselves. Love is rooted in the love God the Father and God the Son have for each other (John 14:15-31).

Jesus even teaches us to love our enemies and persecutors (Mt. 5:43.44), and to sacrifice our lives for brothers and sisters (1 John 3:11-17). The universal scope of the dual commandment of love is already apparent in the Old Testament, when – in line with love of God and neighbour – Israel is instructed to be a light to the world. The LORD calls on Israel to love Him 'with all your heart, with all your soul and with all your strength' (Dt.6:4,5; 10:12; 30:6) and to love your 'neighbour' and the 'stranger' 'as yourself' (Lev.19:18, 34).

4. *Preach*

In addition to the assignments of 'making disciples' and 'teaching', Jesus says that His disciples should 'preach'. This is another aspect of the 'great commission'. In one of His earlier addresses He already told them: 'This gospel of the kingdom will be preached in the whole world' (Mt.24:14). Now, according to Mark 16:15, He said to them: 'preach the good news to all creation'. And in *Luke* 24:47, He declared that in His Name 'to all nations repentance and forgiveness of sins will be preached, beginning at Jerusalem'.

The verb form that is used comes from the Greek verb *kerusso*, which refers to the work of a herald to publicly announce or proclaim the arrival of a king. The herald does so convincingly and with authority. Preaching is not just a compelling message from an earthly monarch. It is a presentation of the gospel, proclaimed on behalf of God, with authority. The same word we find in 2 *Timothy* 4:2: 'Preach the Word'. The preacher experiences that the great commission has been imposed on him by Christ: 'Woe to me if I do not preach the gospel!' (1 Cor.9:16). 'For Christ's love compels us' to the ministry of reconciliation (2 Cor. 5:14, 18).

The preacher is accountable for the binding character of the gospel, which proclaims the victory of King Jesus and announces His glorious arrival. The hearers of that message are informed about the deepest meaning of discipleship. They are called upon as yearning pupils to prepare for the impending arrival of King Jesus, by turning to Him daily in obedience, by confessing their sins and by professing their dependence on Him, by living a new life out of the forgiveness of their sins and peace with God. That basic attitude shows that they are ready to go into the world with the gospel.

5. Be witnesses

In *Matthew* 24:14, Jesus urges the disciples to make the gospel heard as 'a testimony to all nations'. According to Luke in *Acts* 1:8 Jesus says to the disciples: 'You will be My witnesses in Jerusalem and in al Judea and Samaria, and to the ends of the earth'. The Greek nouns used here for 'testimony' and 'witnesses' are respectively *marturion* and *martures* (singular: *marturos*). They refer to the activity of people who are observant and – for example before a court – explain what they have seen or heard or otherwise experienced. The first disciples were eyewitnesses to the work of Jesus. Their successors have not seen Jesus, but they are also witnesses to Him because they have heard from Him by the preaching of their predecessors, the reading of His Word and the work of the Holy Spirit.

In the history of the persecution of Christians in the Roman Empire, the word *martures* was also used as a name for 'martyrs', i.e. those who were put to death because of their testimony of Jesus. Apart from the beheading of John the Baptist, the first martyrs –Stephen and James – fell among Christians in Jerusalem, at the hands of the Jewish leaders. Stephen was killed with help of the later Apostle Paul.

6. *Baptise*

The assignment to baptise is very widely focussed. In *Matthew* 28:19, it follows Jesus' mission to teach all nations: 'baptising them in the name of the Father and of the Son and of the Holy Spirit'. In *Mark* 16:16, prior to the mission to preach *throughout the world*, Jesus says, 'Whoever believes and is baptised will be saved, but whoever does not believe will be condemned'.

The forms of the Greek verb *baptízō* that have been used pertain to 'immersing' in water. In the assignment to baptise, the above mentioned five actions in the great commission return. Baptism is meant to make visible and tangible what Jesus means by: going, making disciples, teaching, preaching and witnessing. Baptism touches the entire message Jesus gives to His disciples. That message is about the whole of His work. The act of immersing in and emerging from the water demonstrates how He humiliated Himself, how He died, and how He rose from the grave. In one symbolic act baptism makes clear the meaning of Christmas, Good Friday and Easter. That is the core of what the disciples of Jesus must learn and what they must pass on to others.

Baptism, often simplified to the act of sprinkling, is at the same time the symbol of the covenant of grace that God made with humanity after the fall in Paradise, which continues until the second coming of Jesus Christ. God's specific covenant with The Old Testament Israel was a temporary demonstration of the universal covenant of grace. That specific covenant also had a symbol, the circumcision of male babies. It indicated the redemption by blood once in Egypt (Ex.12), and it foreshadowed the work of the coming Messiah.

Baptism also refers to the work of Christ, but the expression by many Christians that baptism has taken the place of circumcision[23] does not mean that baptism and circumcision are

---

[23] Cf. a traditional baptism formula in the liturgy of churches of the reformed tradition: Because (under the new covenant) baptism has taken the place of circumcision, infants should be baptized as heirs of the Kingdom of

identical categories, with the latter being replaced by the first. After all, there was nothing left to replace. Circumcision was only performed to males; it was necessary to be incorporated into the people of Israel. In the accomplished work of Christ – according to God's universal plan of salvation – Israel and circumcision have been completely fulfilled and guided to their final goal. They were vague shadows of the covenant of God's grace with the world. In Christ, the reality of God's grace has become visible to all nations. The baptism of men (boys) and women (girls) symbolizes and confirms that reality.[24]

This means that the act of baptism is always meant to take place in a climate of faith in Christ, either personal faith or, prior to that, in the congregation the faith of the believing parents and bystanders concerned. Baptism is an 'outward' or demonstrative affirmation or 'sealing' of the redemption that believers possess in Jesus. It is an objective event that does not depend on the faith of the baptized and the spectators, and also it does not give faith (*ex opere operato*) out of its own effect. But it is a symbolic act that has been instituted by Jesus (Mt.28:19), which calls on every baby and adult to surrender to Him in faith. Therefore, every act of baptism is a public testimony of Christ to the world: a very missionary activity.

c. A concluding promise

Jesus knew that His disciples were weak and limited.[25] They were unable to carry out this great task on their own. For that reason, in the preparatory phase, He had encouraged them to be assured that He was behind them with the omnipotence he had received from His sending Father (Mt.28:18). At the conclusion

---

God and His covenant. Parents are obliged to teach their children in more details about this, when they grow up.

[24] Cf. John Calvin, *Institutes of the Christian Religion,* [transl. Henry Beveridge] Grand Rapids: Eerdmans, 1989, p. 520: 'Baptism serves as our confession before men, inasmuch as it is a mark by which we openly declare that we wish to be ranked among the people of God'.

[25] *Psalm* 103:14-16.

of the mission assignment, He promised that His omnipotence would remain available to them: 'And surely, I am with you always to the very end of the age' (Mt.28:20).

Was it difficult for the disciples to remember 'everything [He] had commanded' them? Yes indeed. That is the very reason why the Holy Spirit is also involved in the great commission. At an earlier stage, Jesus had promised that the Holy Spirit would 'remind' them of all aspects of His commandments (John 14:26). Shortly after His resurrection, upon His first appearance to ten of the disciples, He had blown on them and said to them: 'Receive the Holy Spirit' (Joh.20:22). Soon the Spirit would fully manifest Himself. For that reason, finally, upon the conclusion of the great commission and just before His ascension, Jesus said to them: 'But you will receive the power when the Holy Spirit comes on you' (Acts 1:8).

With those added promises of His omnipotent support and the power of the Spirit, Jesus sent His disciples into the world.

4. The Universal Goal

a. The whole world

God's mission in Jesus Christ has a universal scope. It is aimed at the whole of humanity of all times and all places.[26] From paradise onward, men have been meant to be participants in God's work to restore fallen creation. Men and women are called to testify to God for humanity that has turned its back to Him. Very concretely this was demonstrated when He called Abraham and then Isaac, Jacob and the people of Israel. God's acts with his specifically elected people of Israel was meant to be a missionary spectacle for the whole world. God's grace and judgments were put into practice in the history of Old Testament Israel. By this God wanted to break the stubborn unbelief of Israel itself and of the world's population.

In *Acts* 3 Peter shows this great universal perspective to his Jewish audience. The Prophet announced by Moses is Jesus. 'You must listen to everything He tells you' (3:22; cf. Dt.18:15). In Him 'all peoples on earth will be blessed' (3:25; cf. Gen.22:18; Gal.3:8). The Kingdom of God has come in principle and will come in its completeness. This determines the preaching and the ministry of Jesus. After all, the teaching of all nations is about the all-encompassing restoration of all things (Acts 3:21).

The Old Testament nation of Israel had not been able to carry out this universal mission. Partly because of this, the world had not met with God as He is according to His special revelation. Consequently, humanity remained in darkness con-

---

[26] Donald Senior & Carroll Stuhlmueller, *The Biblical Foundations for Mission*, London: SCM Press, 1984, p. 339,340, under the heading 'A universal God' points to the universal sovereignty of God, which is the source and measure of worldwide mission: 'Thus the Biblical God is the ultimate source of mission and the ultimate catalyst to the church's instinct to move beyond the boundaries of a particular culture or national group'. He 'stands as the final seal on our common humanity'. 'The deepest impulse of biblical religion is that the God of Israel and the God of Jesus is the God of everyone'.

cerning the way of salvation. But according to God's plan, His only begotten Son Jesus Christ, as a man, has fulfilled the mission of Israel and disclosed its essential significance for the world, including Israel itself. At His incarnation, He declared Himself willing to fulfill Israel's place in revelation history. He is the fulfilment of the Old Testament sacrifices that characterized the function of Israel (Hebr.10). In Christ, Israel came to its true destiny. The same goes for its mission. With His arrival to the 'lost sheep of Israel' (Mt.15:24), He demonstrates His saving intention for the lost of the whole world. Performing Israel's universal task has become possible in Jesus Christ. He passed that great assignment to His disciples and then to all believers in the church/congregation of all places and times.

The universal nature of Jesus' mission is reflected in several ways in the words He has used to describe its purpose:

(1) He speaks in concrete *geographical* terms: 'the world' (John 3:16; 1 John1:9), 'the whole world' (Mt.24:14; Mk.16:15), 'to the ends of the earth' (Acts 1:8; cf. Ps.67:11).

(2) He also speaks in inclusive *demographic* terms: 'all nations' (Mt. 24:14; 28:19; Lk.24:47), 'all creation' (Mk.16:15). *Matthew* 28:19, via the family register in 1:1-17, directly connects with the promise to Abraham in *Genesis* 12:3 (cf. Ps.67:3-6), 'all peoples on earth'.

(3) He also puts the mission in an *eschatological* perspective. Participation in the mission of Jesus culminates in His Second Coming: 'And the gospel of the kingdom will be preached in the whole world, as a testimony to all nations; and then the end will come' (Mt.24:14). 'And surely I am with you always, to the very end of the age' (Mt.28:20).

(4) Finally, Jesus involves in his mission the universally existing categories of people who seem to have the 'the least' value in general opinion: 'the poor', 'the broken-hearted', 'the prisoners', 'the blind', 'the oppressed' (Lk.4:18,19; cf. Is. 61:1,2), the 'hungry', the 'thirsty', the 'strangers', the 'naked', the 'sick', those 'in prison' (Mt.:25:31-46), 'the lame', 'those who have leprosy', 'the deaf', 'the dead', and again 'the poor' (Mt.11:5).

Showing an apparent preference for the 'the poor', Jesus makes them the target of his mission: 'the good news is preached to the poor'. And meaningfully, He urges us not to be annoyed with Him due to His choosing the destitute: 'Blessed is the man who does not fall away on account of Me'.[27]

b. The nations and the religions

The universal and inclusive scope of the great commission to the first disciples and their successors means that they had been dealing with peoples and cultures not familiar with the Holy Scripture in which God revealed Himself. The true knowledge of God had often been at a low level even within Israel, let alone the usually pitch-black darkness of ignorance outside Israel among the peoples.

Yet the Bible indicates that from creation onward God has kept the nations in mind and that He has not let Himself be without testimony among them (Acts 14:16,17). In the nature that was created by Him, He has always shown to all peoples something about who He is. Moreover, the peoples of the Middle East were intertwined with the history of God's revelation to the people of Israel. The fact that God was known among them is evidenced by Biblical examples. But there are also extra-biblical indications of a certain knowledge of the only true God in the great number of cultures of the nations around the world. This shows that God had not only prepared the gospel for all nations, but that He has also prepared the peoples to receive and accept the gospel. Let us dwell on some examples.

Don Richardson started his life as a missionary in Irian Jaya. Subsequently, he studied the cultures of peoples who accepted Islam and then faced the gospel. He is convinced that God uses elements of the cultures of nations to draw people to Himself and that in this way He fulfils *Ecclesiastes* 3:11:

---

[27] Mt.11:5; cf. Mt.5:3; Ps.70:6; James 5:2. David J. Bosch, *Transforming Mission: Paradigm Shifts in Theology of Mission*, New York: Maryknoll, 1993, p. 98-122, observes a special missionary target particularly with Luke, directed at the poor and also at the rich: 'Gospel for de Poor – and the Rich'.

'He [God] has made everything beautiful in its time. He has also set eternity in the hearts of men; yet they cannot fathom what God has done from beginning to end'.[28]

Here the question arises: Of what value are the many religions in the world and their associated cultures, ideologies, and philosophies of life.[29] According to atheist thinkers, this question is no longer relevant. In the modern reality of science and technology, many have abolished religion as an explanation for what people are and can essentially be. Western atheists have also influenced some opinion-makers outside Europe and America with that idea. Here we refer to some negative aspects of the rich powerful Western countries, which influence the developing world overseas. Westerners seem to think, that they are autonomous, in control of their world, and don't need help from God or anyone else. They are teaching other cultures their messages of atheism – leading people to believe that God is irrelevant – self-sufficiency, wanton greed, and deviancy, A connected aspect is the dictatorship of relativism which dominates the Western world today. Under the guise of tolerance these societies are becoming the most intolerant in the world. Now these powers are forcing others to accept their moral code, using their leverage to force a new unchristian or even anti-Christian agenda on economically weaker powers.

An example of Western atheist influence is the South African philosopher Charles Gwena. In his book *Africanness*, he has given a multifaceted description of the identity of African man and culture. But Gwena does not mention any connection between African identity and religion. He silently acts

---

[28] Don Richardson, 'A World Prepared for the Gospel: The Melchizedek Factor', in: *Eternity in Their Hearts*, Minneapolis: Bethany House, 2014 (first 1981), p.9-136. A similar conclusion, although in a South American context (Surinam) is drawn by: Kees van der Ziel, *Kom uit je wigwam: in de kraamkamer van een bijbelvertaalproject bij de Karaiben*, Barnabas, 2000.

[29] C.J. Haak, *Gereformeerde Missiologie en Oecumenica: Beknopt overzicht aan het begin van de 21ste eeuw A.D.*, Zwolle: De Verre Naasten, 2005, p.140,141, a brief introduction to the study of religions, with useful references to relevant literature.

from the untenable assumption that God does not exist or does not matter. On African Christianity he only says that it is an imitation of the violence of colonial powers.[30] However, African identity has been characterized by a traditional monotheistic religiosity with origins in Antiquity. This has remained an important trait of 'Africanness'. Moreover, Christianity has gained numerical majority in Africa after the colonial era. Religions are alive and popular in the indigenous societies all over the world, except in secularized Western culture.

How do religions relate to the Christian faith? How should missionaries deal with the religions and their believers? Let us particularly look at the followers of the Jewish religion (Judaism) and Islam. Together with Christianity they are considered to be the so-called 'Abrahamic' religions, which are characterized by monotheism. We also think of other monotheistic religions, which have developed among the original populations of the continents to which missionaries were called, for example the 'American Native Religions' (NTR) and the 'African Traditional Religion' (ATR). Apart from those, we look at the polytheistic religions such as Hinduism, and religious systems such as Buddhism and Shintoism. Many followers of the world of religions also adhere to all kinds of folk beliefs and animism, such as fate, witches, spirits and animism, and the worshipping of ancestors. Finally, there is a multitude of more or less religiously coloured philosophical and ideological systems.[31]

The great commission of Jesus does not include concrete instructions on religions. But Jesus, who sent His disciples to the very ends of the earth, said of Himself, 'I am the Way, and the Truth, and Life. No one comes to the Father ex-

---

[30] Charles Ngwena, *What is Africanness?: Contesting nativism in race, culture and sexualities*, Pretoria University Law Press, 2018, p.63-65.

[31] J. Verkuijl, *Contemporary Missiology: An Introduction*, Grand Rapids: Eerdmans, 1978, 373-404: 'A Study and Evaluation of Ideologies in the Developing Countries'. Cf. Steven Paas, *Christianity in Eurafrica: A History of the Church in Europe and Africa*, Washington DC; New Academia Publishing, 2017, p.43-48, 289-304.

cept through Me' (John 14:6). How should we use this text in modern debates on religious pluralism? Certain religions, for example Islam, did not exist in the time of Jesus. The whole concept of 'religion' was not yet used in the meaning we attach to it in the modern age.[32] In its context, the passage seems to be mainly about Jesus applying certain concepts in the Torah (e.g. *Psalm* 119: way, truth, life) to Himself. Nevertheless, this is a statement in which Jesus takes the central place as the way to God. We will show that this does not imply all there is to be said about the truth claims of religions or about the eternal fate of those who have never heard of Jesus.

At least, the way of salvation does not make a detour skipping Christ. The Apostle Peter confirmed that when for the Jewish Sanhedrin he accounted for his being a disciple of Jesus, whose mission he carried out: 'Salvation is found in no-one else, for there is no other name under heaven given to men by which we must be saved' (Acts 4:12). That exclusive claim clearly indicates a limit. Outside of Christ, God cannot be reached. This implies that the disciples and their successors, when encountering the religions of the world receive the responsibility to bear witness of the unique and irreplaceable position of their Sender. This leads them to the question of just how to approach religions theoretically and practically. Should this be done in an open, dismissive or pragmatic way?

Let us consider the suggestion that religions and their related cultures are useful to missionaries as a stepping stone to make people find God as He has been revealed in Scripture. The question then is whether the great commission leaves room for the idea that religions can help people to get to know the Way, the Truth and the Life, that is Jesus.

This is not about the contention that all religions basically are ways that lead to God. Such a multiple ways theory

---

[32] Peter Harrison, *The Territories of Science and Religion*, University of Chicago, 2017, p.7-9: The concept 'religion' that we know as doctrine of salvation, theology, dogmatics, tradition, originates in the Modern Age (after the Middle Ages). Before that time the word also existed, but its meaning was different: piety, mode of worship, fulfilling obligations, etc.

eliminates the uniqueness of Christ and should be rejected because of the just mentioned limit.[33]

Here we are considering the view that religions contain elements of truth, which are somehow of value for carrying out the mission of Jesus. According to this popular conviction, there are similarities or overlaps between the different religions and the Christian faith. However, such an hypothesis cannot be proven or rejected as a matter of course. This is evident from the theological discussion about 'points of contact'[34] between Christianity and other religions, which started more than a century ago. By definition Christians are engaged in mission. This often gets them in touch with adherents of other religions. Therefore, we cannot circumvent this issue.

The debate on 'points of contact' began in the West, where mission organizations and politicians tried to determine their attitude towards the non-Christian religions in the colonies. It became more urgent as Western society itself became more multi-cultural through globalisation and refugee migration. Essentially, the question pertains to Christianity all over the world. Sanders wrote a fascinating and clarifying essay on the issue.[35] In fact, there are three positions: denial, overvaluation, two-sidedness.

c. The denial of points of contact

First, there are those who think that there are no points of contact. They are supposed not to not exist because the Christian faith is different in every way. This is the opinion of the influ-

---

[33] Kees van der Ziel, discusses the limits of contextualization, in the article: 'Door het oog van de naald. Cultuur, context en bijbelvertaling bij de Karaiben', in: *Wereld en Zending. Tijdschrift voor Interculturele theologie*. Jrg. 31, 2003, p. 47-60.

[34] The term 'points of contact' I derive from: Isabel Apawo Phiri and Dietrich Werner (chief editors), *Anthology of African Christianity*, Oxford: Regnum Books, 2016, p.91, 103. The authors also use the terms 'meeting points' (p.97) and 'points of interface (p.999). Cf. my review article in: *The Ecumenical Review*, WCC, November 2019, p.245-248.

[35] E. Sanders, 'A Theological Study of Point of Contact Theory', in: *Global Missiology*, Contemporary Practice, July, 2004 [Internet]

ential theologian Karl Barth (1886-1968). Between the two world wars of the twentieth century he defended this theory in his discussion with Emil Brunner (1889-1966). Alister McGrath has written a clarifying overview of the visions of both theologians.[36] With his denial of points of contact with Christianity in *all* cultures, including his own German culture, Barth wanted to emphasize God's special grace, which can only be found in Christ. He radically opposed bridges to God from man's own cultural endeavours. 'God Himself creates a connection', he said. By this, Barth meant that the preaching of the gospel itself, as an independent downward movement from God, creates a bridge.

But Barth denies or undervalues God's general grace for all, believers and unbelievers. We have to acknowledge that after man's fall into sin, darkness has not become all-controlling. God has left us some light. He left remainders of the original goodness and righteousness of His creation. These beautiful patches of light are visible because of the splendour of nature. They can also be visible in the cultures and religious representations of people and in science. However, Barth's verdict on the supposed points of contact can be understood when one realizes that he had to stand up to 19th-century Enlightenment thinkers who denied the exclusivity of the way of salvation in Christ and had to oppose the racially coloured idea of the 'Volkschristianisierung' (christianization of the whole German people) and the 'folk's identity', in other words the idea that Christianity could be defined from the bottom up, from the nature of a nation.

Barth did not really take into account that his denial of the existence of points of light in foreign cultures and religions could be abused in the climate of Enlightenment liberalism and Western superiority thinking, which he abhorred. That climate was the product of many centuries of cooperation between state

---

[36] Alister E. McGrath, 'Natural Theology? The Barth – Brunner Debate of 1934' [Internet]. I.P.C. van 'Hof, *Het zendingsbegrip van Karl Bart*, Hoenderloo: Zendingsstudieraad, 1946, p.12-66.

and church in a 'corpus christianum', aimed at expanding power. In the 19th century, such thinking supported the rise of racial theories, imperialism and colonialism.

For this reason, Barth did not have many followers among the members of the young Christianity that had arisen during colonialism. Christians of the subjugated indigenous peoples remained inclined to value their own traditional religions more positively than the Barthian oriented missionaries did. Founded in 1963, the ecumenical organization All Africa Conference of Churches (AACC) regarded indigenous religions as God-willed religious insights, which would be a pre-stage or a preparation for the advent of the gospel. At the same time, this explains why many non-Western young Christians missed the Barthian antidote against religious liberalism and became vulnerable to the influences by certain theologians and philosophers from the West who regard all religions as ways to the same goal.

However, this influence was not generally effective. This is shown by the example of the Nigerian evangelical theologian Byang Kato (1936-1975). In his radical rejection of the possibility of points of contact, he was close to Karl Barth. The theologian Kpobi says that Kato studied the traditional religions of Africa, only with the aim of proving that they were false and idolatries. He didn't treat them as *praeparatio evangelica*.[37] Kato feared that a liberal approach to traditional religions would undermine the unique christocentric meaning and authority of the Bible, paving the way for syncretism, i.e. a mixing of religions.

---

[37] Byang H. Kato, *Theological Pitfalls in Africa*, University of Virginia: Evangelical Publ. House, 1975. Cf. Yusufu Turaki, *Foundations of African Traditional Religion and Worldview*, Nairobi: Word Alive, 2006. Cf. Christina Maria Breman, *The Associaton of Evangelicals in Africa*, Zoetermeer: Boekencentrum, 1996, p. 383-399, 430-432, 532. Cf. David N.A. Kpobi, 'Evangelicals and African Ecumenism', in: Phiri en Werner, *Anthology*, p.838. See also: Birgit Meyer, 'Christianity in Africa: From African Independent to Pentecostal-Charismatic Churches', in: *Annual Review of Anthropology*, Vol. 33 (2004), p. 447-474.

d. The overvaluing of points of contact

Secondly, we consider the opinion that religions have points of contact or common ground with the Christian faith, which would have some salvific quality. This is a popular thought, cherished by many modern Western and non-Western theologians. It is believed that there is more continuity than discontinuity in the relationship between the Christian faith and other beliefs. Here are some examples from the African context: Kwame Bediako believes that God – now proclaimed by the missionaries – was already worshipped in African traditional religions. Before the missionaries thought they had introduced Christianity in Africa, the Africans already knew and worshipped the true God. African theologians like John S. Mbiti and E.B. Idowu claim that Christianity and African traditional religions share many things, such as the concept of God, morality and community sentiments.[38] These theologians observe aspects of alienation from their own culture within Western Christianity and they argue that indigenous religions are a vital source for strengthening Christian theology. They are guided by the assumption of continuity, in which Christianity fulfils the religious desires found in indigenous religions.

That is why Mbiti argues that indigenous religions have contributed to the rapid spread of Christianity. In his opinion, there are many parallels between the characteristics of God in the Bible and those in traditional religion. In fact, he believes that the indigenous religions essentially recognize the same God as the God described in the Bible. According to him, traditional believers do not experience stumbling blocks when in their indigenous faith they move to the faith as proposed in Scripture. Essentially, they don't change faith. They consider the Word of God in the Bible as the Word of the same God they know by the African religion.[39] So much for Mbiti.

---

[38] John S. Mbiti, 'Foreword', in: Phiri en Werner, *Anthology*, p. xvii-xxi.

[39] John S. Mbiti, *Introduction to African Traditional Religion*, Nairobi: East African Educational Publications, p.180,189,190. Vgl. Tabona Shoko, 'Christianity and Traditional African Religions', in: Phiri en Werner, *Anthology*, p. 91.

As Mbiti particularly speaks with regard to the African Traditional Religion (s) (ATR), others, refer to for example the American Indigenous Religions (American Native Religions – ANR), Islam and the Jewish religion (Judaism).

Richard Twiss is convinced that the one and only God of the Bible, who has made everything, is also present in the religions of the 'First Nations', the indigenous peoples of America. He does not imply that all religious expressions before or outside Christianity are equally valid. He particularly refers to the peoples and religions that are not animistic, but honour the one and unique God as Creator. According to Twiss, the one Creator reveals Himself in and through a multitude of cultural realities in humans and other beings. God uses those creatures in the whole of our 'Mother Earth', which they respect. Twiss wants to distance himself from the 'American Christian mythology' of Western white culture, which comes from colonization and paternalism. As a follower of Jesus, he embraces theological perspectives of indigenous Christian leaders, who want to go new ways of contextualization, in which justice is done to indigenous cultural and spiritual values and rituals.[40] In those cultures he sees common ground with Christianity. In fact, he says that elements of indigenous religion can go hand in hand with the Christian faith in a kind of sanctified 'syncretism' (mixing of religions). Twiss realises the danger of going to the extreme, because at the same time in a posture of 'counter-syncretism' he wants to shield himself from certain dark elements in indigenous culture that weaken, contradict, or end faith in Jesus. He considers himself warned by Western Christianity, which was corrupted by mixing with the world of violence, power and money, thus opening the door to secularization.[41]

Of the non-Christian religions, Islam, as a related monotheistic religion, may have most or at least the most important

---

[40] Twiss, 'The Creator's Presence Among Native People', in: *Rescuing the Gospel from the Cowboys*, p.16, 17.

[41] Twiss, 'The Colonization, Evangelization and Assimilation of First Nations People', in: *Rescuing the Gospel from the Cowboys*, p.18-92.

points of contact with the Christian faith. The Koran refers to Jesus in a positive way, and quite often, namely in 93 *ayat* (verses), divided into 15 *suras* (chapters). It reports that He healed the sick, gave life to the death, was born from the virgin Mary, preached the gospel to the Jews and was sent by Allah as a prophet. In the Koran Jesus receives power from the Holy Spirit, and He is called 'Word of God' and 'Messiah'. The Koran also respectfully mentions the *Torah* (Taurat), the *Psalms* (Zabur) and the *Gospel* (Injil), although it is said that Christians have forged those holy books. Some Christians and many Muslims embrace these impressive points of contact and suggest that they indicate a shared truth about God. Some missionaries classify the transition of converts from Islam to Christianity in six stages (C1-C6) of increasing rapprochement to the Christian faith.[42] From step to step converts are integrating in some way their cultural and religious traditions into their newly found Christian identity. In general, it is realised that it is important to continue to make distinctions. The new identity requires a conscious choice for Christ, i.e. conversion. It is therefore not possible that at some stage the faith of Islam will essentially flow towards the Christian faith. Somewhere, at the point of surrendering to Christ, there is a break. In retrospect, the convert sees that the initially observed 'overlap 'between the original religion loses much of his shining truth through the unique light of Christ.

Fully recognizing certain similarities concerning Jesus, we must realize that the Koran does not give Him a decisive position. Islam is positioning Jesus behind Muhammad, who is said to be the 'Seal of All Prophets'. The Koran presents Jesus as a defender of Islam and a prominent forerunner of Muhammad, to whom He would have surrendered His place. How come that Islam has such a twisted image of Jesus Christ? I agree with Kenneth Cragg, who believes that much of the

---

[42] M. Coleman en P Verster, 'Contextualisation of the Gospel among Muslims', in: *Acta Theologica*, 2006 (nr.2), p. 94-115.

file:///C:/Users/Gebruiker/Downloads/49037-65096-1-PB.pdf

'Muslim unawareness of Christ' has been caused by unbiblical preaching and bad examples of Christians.[43] The true Jesus is not entirely unknown to Muslims and at the same time He was not known to them at all. For Cragg the wrong image of Jesus is the main justification of mission among Muslims. We must restore to them what has gone wrong with the Christian information about Jesus Christ.

Undoubtedly, most Western Christians feel more related to Jewish religion, or Judaism. We are used to talking about our 'Judeo-Christian' culture. Anyway, we share with the Jews an important part of the Bible. Many believe that Jews and Christians serve the same God. However, it remains to be seen how many of this supposedly common ground holds. History writer Tom Holland thinks the Jewish faith is closer to Islam than to Christianity.[44] We should also consider the Jewish *talmudic* tradition,[45] which implies the rejection of the New Testament and of Jesus as the Son of God and as Messiah. We cannot escape the conclusion that Jews and Christians explain the Bible very differently. Jews themselves consider the Christian faith as a 'different religion'. In Chapter 5, we will investigate what that means for the mission of Jesus.

e. The two-sidedness of the points of contact

An evaluation of the points of contact or common ground between the religions and the Christian faith requires a qualification in the light of God's revelation in the Scriptures. In my

---

[43] Kenneth Cragg, *The Call of the Minaret*, New York: Orbis Books/ Maryknoll and Ibadan: Daystar Press, 1985³, p. 218-242

[44] Tom Holland, the author of the epoch-making book *Dominion* (see bibliography), in an interview with Dick Schinkelshoek, in: *Nederlands Dagblad*, 27-2-2020, says the term Judeo-Christian is a nonsense word ('onzinwoord'), because the Jewish answer to the question about God's will with us looks much more (stukken meer') to the the Muslim perception than to the view of Christians.

[45] De *Talmud* (consisting of the *Mishna* and the *Gemara*) and the *Midrash* are post-Biblical Jewish writings, which are very influential in defending rabbinical interpretation of the *Tanakh* (Old Testament), and reject the New Testament.

opinion, the Bible gives no reason to deny the existence of points of contact. Moreover, the Bible does not require us to interpret them only negatively – possibly as a consequence of confusion or fear of the unknown. We should admit that beautiful and positive things also exist in people and religions beyond the reach of the gospel. Those things do not stand apart from God, but they have to do with His goodness. Many indigenous peoples have held a vaguely monotheistic image, that is the memory of the existence of the one God.[46] The names they use to refer to Him can reflect the work and name of the true and only God.[47]

We also recognize that beautiful things have been left in the previously 'Christian' Western culture that has now been secularized to a great extent. But at the same time, we should admit that in practice the West – including its religious aspects – has often shown less of God's appreciation for man and nature than some 'pagan' cultures.

Anyway, God has left elements of truth and beauty in religions that preceded or existed parallel to Christianity, which could sometimes make Western people jealous. During years of contact with African traditions, my wife and I have often observed a level of civilization in the poorest 'heathen' huts, which often is higher than is shown by the rich modern Western ways of life. For example, the widely accepted practice of 'ulemu' in the Malawian tradition offers many splendid forms of courtesy, respect to the elderly and reverence to God.[48] Stephen Msiska,

---

[46] Cf. Richardson, 'The Vague God', in: *Eternity*, p.9-64.

[47] In Malawi I found many names for God that are (also) used by Christians. The most famous name is: *Mulungu* (divine being). Other names are: *Chiuta/ Chauta* (the great celestial arc); *Leza* (the foresayer, the lightning); *Mlengi* (the creator, the cause of all in life); *Mlezi* (the sustainer, the one who feeds all); *Mphambe/ Mphambi* (the almighty, apparent from thunder and lightning); *Namalenga* (the creator); *Uluhlanga* (the origin, the source); *Umkhulu kakhulu* (the greatest of all); *Umkhulumgango* (the great designer); *Umnikazi we zinthu zonke* (the owener of all things); Unkulunkulu (the great one). See my *Oxford Chichewa Dictionary*: https://translate.chichewadictionary.org/

[48] The word *ulemu* comes from Chichewa, a language spoken in Malawi, parts of Zambia, Mozambique and Zimbabwe. It has a rich meaning:

a Malawian pastor, called these points of light 'golden buttons' He bemoaned the fact that Western missionaries had totally rejected all aspects of the African religion when they brought Christianity, throwing out the good with the bad. He maintained that there were remaining elements of beauty and truth.[49]

The great commission of Jesus cannot be carried out without acknowledging the positive and – by Biblical standards – possibly loftier aspects of the receiving cultures. Kroesbergen draws to our attention 'the language of faith'. The way Africans speak about the world of spirits and powers and their holistic worldview is perceived as strange in Europe and America.[50] But these perspectives often connect more to a Biblical view of man and world than the Enlightenment ideas, which have come to control Western culture.

The most important question is why and to which end God has left elements of truth, law and beauty to exist in the extra-biblical religions and cultures. Do these remnants of divine light in religions have a healing quality out of themselves, which is salvific to people? I am convinced that the Bible answers this question in the negative. I wrote this sentence after reading the pericope *Romans* 1:18-32. The general knowledge of God in the religions does not in itself lead to Christ. Essential knowledge of the living God does not exist outside Jesus Christ. Salvation is only there in Him. These religions do not know Him, at least not as He has been revealed in Scripture.[51]

1.politeness; 2.courtesy; 3.honor; 4.esteem; 5.reverence; 6.etiquette; 7.respect; 8.00; 9.integrity; 10.dignity, 11.glory. See: *Oxford Chichewa Dictionary*, https://translate.chichewadictionary.org/

[49] Stephen Kauta Msiska, *Golden Buttons: Christianity and Traditional Religion among the Tumbuka*, Blantyre: Christian Literature Association of Malawi, 1997.

[50] Hermen Kroesbergen, *The Language of Faith in Southern Africa: Spirit World, Power, Community, Holism*, Cape Town: AOSIS, 2019.

[51] See my discussion on African Traditional Religion(s), in: *Christianity in Eurafrica,* p.25-28 ('Characteristics of African Historiography'), p.295-296 (African Traditional Religion), p.507-514 (Conversion in Africa, the 'Continuum' and Calvin, etc.).

This also applies if the Christian faith has degenerated, distancing itself from the Bible and God, to become a cultural religion of nominal Christians who do not (want to) know Christ Himself. Although Scripture leaves room for recognizing continuity, initially and most importantly there is discontinuity. Non-Christian religions[52] have traces of the law of God (Rom.2: 14.15) on the one hand, but on the other hand, because of the failure to recognize Christ, they have twisted the image of God and in the final analysis they stand against Him (Eph. 2:2,3,12; Eph.4: 18.19).

This interpretation of Scripture is not an invention of 19th-century Western missionaries and agents of colonialism in their encounter with the indigenous religions of America, Africa and Asia, but it was defended a long time before, for example, by the 16th-century Reformer John Calvin.[53] In His general grace, God has left glittering 'sparks' of righteousness in His fallen creation, including human nature and natural religions. These 'sparks' in themselves do not lead to rebirth or conversion; they are not healing, not even partially. On the contrary, instead of receiving peace with God, the unconverted man of the religions experiences serious discontent. Based on his mission experience Richardson characterizes that situation as 'doubly haunted', besieged by scary spirits from two sides. First, those men and women feel eternity as a strange, vague, uncertain destination. At the same time, the law of God, which is written in their hearts, says that they will miss their eternal destiny.[54] Right next to the spots of light that God has left, the darkness of Satan prevails, in the phenomena of black magic, witchcraft, double-heartedness, infidelity, lying, and immorality. The remnant of the original light gives the natural man knowledge of God's law.

But that knowledge does not serve to find stepping stones to salvation outside Christ. On the contrary! Natural men

---

[52] See footnote in chapter 4, section b.

[53] Calvin, *Institutes*, especially: I,3,1.

[54] Richardson, 'Peoples with strange customs', in: *Eternity*, p.99.

and women who know about God's 'eternal power and divine nature' (Rom.1:20) and who do not convert to Him cannot benefit from that knowledge in the last judgment. God leaves to them some original light of creation in order to deprive them of all the apologies they would like to offer, attempting to make it acceptable that they did not repent and accept Christ as their Saviour.[55]

Possibly, that warning especially concerns nominal Christians, Muslims and Jews (Judaists), who are closest to the fire of truth on the altar, which God has bestowed on humanity in the Scriptures, but have extinguished it or took 'unauthorized fire' to it (cf. Lev.10:1-7), or like the heathen have 'suppressed the truth by their wickedness' (Rom.1:18). The reality of this warning emphasizes the great seriousness of the great commission.

The beauty of the points of contact, however, is that they are also used by the Holy Spirit. Through the work of the Spirit in their hearts, Christ is always with the missionaries. He teaches them to gain insight into these remaining light spots among the recipients of the gospel. Missionaries must study in depth the culture and religious situation in which they work. Knowing, appreciating and using points of contact is necessary. It is part of the loving and respectful missionary approach of fellow human beings, who do not yet know Christ. Then the Holy Spirit will make Christians discover how He wants to use those points of contact among the recipients as entrances, pegs or hooks for the message of the gospel to get hold. Points of contact serve the missionaries as tools to proclaim the miracle through which people get to know Jesus as their Saviour and convert to Him.

---

[55] Rom.1:20. Cf. 'Mankind's Guilty Knowledge of God', in: *New Geneva Study Bible: Bringing the Light of Reformation to Scripture*, Nelson, p.1767: 'In one sense, fallen humanity does not know God, since what people believe about the objects of their worship, falsifies and distorts the truth about God. In another sense all human beings do know God, but in guilt, with uncomfortable inklings of the judgment they cannot avoid. Only the gospel of Christ can speak peace to this aspect of the human condition'.

This miracle, which the Spirit of Christ performs in human beings, is related to the forensic (i.e. from external origin) character of faith and to the imputed nature of Christ's redeeming work. In the obedience of faith, lost people accept Jesus has paid for their sin and taken their place, and that He bestows on them the righteousness and holiness required by God. That is the reality of the joyful message, which shows how much people – as long as they are trapped in religions without Christ – live in darkness and without hope, apart from all the possible points of contact. This reality once again emphasizes the great missionary responsibility, which all Christians have received, in one way or another.

5. Beginning at Jerusalem

a. The geographical and cultural significance

Jesus wanted the disciples to begin their missionary activities 'at Jerusalem'. This is explicitly mentioned by the evangelist Luke (Lk.24:47). In *Acts* 1:8, the same Luke writes that Jesus wanted the disciples to begin their work 'in' Jerusalem and that He also involved the area adjacent to the city: 'in Jerusalem and in all Judea and Samaria'. What did Jesus mean by this instruction, for the disciples and for us?

This is first about the geographical and cultural significance of 'Jerusalem'. Jesus consciously wanted them to start their work nearby, in their own city and country. He did not want the remaining eleven disciples, later supplemented by Matthias (Acts 1:26), to immediately undertake distant journeys to proclaim the gospel in foreign regions and to other peoples. In chapter 1, we noted that after the ascension of Jesus the universal dimension of His mission would be soon on the agenda; it began at the Feast of Pentecost in *Acts* 2 and by Paul's calling in *Acts* 9. But first the disciples had to focus on their own environment.

That explicit instruction was given by Jesus for a special reason. Perhaps the disciples did not find Jerusalem and its surroundings the most logical place for the start of their missionary work. Perhaps they were afraid to be public witnesses to Jesus in their own familiar context. After all, their wandering with Jesus had shown how dangerous that was. The Jews had manipulated the Romans in order to have Jesus killed, and now they were boiling with hostility against the followers of Jesus. The air was full of the spirit of hatred and persecution. This was sufficient reason to be apprehensive and – at least initially – to look for safer target areas.

But Jesus just wanted them to start in their own Jewish cultural and religious environment. Because they were best prepared for the spreading of the gospel in their own familiar context. Their knowledge of the geography, language, customs and religious beliefs of the Jewish people made them the most suitable missionary partakers to find points of contact for the proclamation of the gospel in and near Jerusalem. There were no cultural barriers that would prevent them from being understood. This is not to say that such advantages were a guarantee of success, since their Jewish identity actually triggered spiritual obstacles among their fellow Jews all the sooner. That is shown by the sequence of events. The Jewish leaders may have understood the message, but instead of repenting, they burned with anger and started to persecute the disciples and their followers. The first Christian congregation had to flee and spread in areas around the Mediterranean. That stimulated the speed and thoroughness with which, some time later, the gospel was spread outside Canaan.

Jesus' selection for the starting point of missionary activities contains an important lesson for today in our Western culture. Jesus indicates that for us as well missionary work first of all begins next door, in our relationship with our neighbours. That is not easy. Because like the first disciples, Christians are in danger of colliding with the familiar climate of their own country and people. Active local Christians are sometimes more vulnerable than the classic Western missionary, who works in distant countries among peoples who are economically and politically dependent on the West. Functioning as living witnesses of Christ in one's own environment is risky. Caution and tact are required. Christians sometimes experience decreasing tolerance when they desire to pass on something of the gospel in their daily practice. It may then be good to wonder whether resistance or even enmity has been aroused by their own attitude or by the nature of the message. Sometimes, Christians in a Western context may feel that their own freedom and security are under pressure. However, we should not be afraid, because Jesus still maintains the promise of His missional words to the disciples: 'And surely I am with you always, to the very end of the age' (Mt.28:20). He is the One who has been sent, and therefore confidently and calmly we take part in His mission.

The second lesson for us is that, like the disciples of that time, we must first carefully, respectfully and with love utilize the openings our own culture offers. This is all the more urgent because Europe and America have become real mission fields, more than the continents where Christianity is growing. We should pay attention to the patches of light and truth that God has left in our traditions through His general grace and we should look for cultural 'hooks' to which the gospel can be fastened. The Jewish people of the time of the first disciples knew a lot about God, although many twisted and abused that knowledge. Our Western culture still contains remnants of a centuries-old Christian tradition. That enables secularized Western men and women to recognize the message of the gospel, even if they decide to reject it. The use of these beautiful remains in our culture can provide Christians with a special sensitivity and ability to make the gospel land among contemporary Europeans and Americans, even if that message runs against the mainstream of cultural developments.

b. Important in the history of revelation

The starting position of 'Jerusalem' in the great commission of Jesus is not only determined by geography and culture, but also by its roots in the history of God's revelation, i.e. in how God has revealed in the Bible who He is and what He wants from us. Jesus wants His first disciples to begin at the city of Jerusalem in order to connect the proclamation of the gospel to the entire Old Testament from the description of paradise onward.[56]

After all, before God made His covenant with Abraham in *Genesis* 15, which was followed by His special relationship with the patriarchs of Israel, Jerusalem as a 'city of peace' was already a demonstration of God's merciful intentions for the world. Melchizedek (literally: king of righteousness) is the key figure who connects God's covenant of mercy with humanity from Paradise to Christ. Especially in Abraham's meeting with

---

[56] Cf. Bosch, *Transforming Mission,* p.93-97, 'Jerusalem – The Jews first and to the Gentiles'.

King Melchizedek, God shows that the line of Abraham (cf. Gen.12:1,2 and Mt. 1:1-17) and the other patriarchs through Israel to Christ is subordinate to the line of Melchizedek to Christ. Christ was not the High Priest according to the order of Levi, which was limited to Israel, but He is the eternal and universal High Priest in the order of Melchizedek (Gen. 14: 18-20; Ps. 110; Hebr. 5: 5-10; 6:19,20; 7:1-21). Melchizedek's Jerusalem reaches higher than Israel's Jerusalem. Both are used by God. The Jerusalem of Melchizedek directly points to God's universal acts with all mankind in Christ. Therefore, the meeting between Abraham and Melchizedek, poetically represented in *Psalm* 110, is a signal of the profound christocentric meaning of the Old Testament. Jesus confirms that in *Matthew* 22:43-45 where He applies the words of *Psalm* 110 to Himself.

Some believe that emphasizing the christocentric (God the Son) character of the Old Testament, as was done by the reformer Martin Luther,[57] would be at the expense of the theocentric (God the Father) nature of it. However, only in the light of Christ can we know who God is in both testaments. Jesus said: 'No-one comes to the Father except through Me ... Anyone who has seen Me has seen the Father' (John 14:6-9). Although the concepts of theocentricity and christocentricity indicate the distinction between the Father and the Son, they cannot be played against each other because of their unity.[58] A christocentric interpretation of Scripture is aimed at making clear that the tri-une God is at the centre.

---

[57] Paas, *Luther on Jews and Judaism*, p.7-25.

[58] C.P. de Boer has contrasted those two terms, at the presentation of his dissertation *Christos Sunthronos* (Theological University Apeldoorn, January 2020). He investigated New Testament references to Psalm 110. While acknowledging that in *Matthew* 22:44 Jesus interprets this Psalm messianically, applying it to Himself, yet De Boer relativates the Psalm's immediate christocentric significance, consequently also Melchizedek's place in it. He says: I am standing by an historic approach that is mainly theocentric and not christocentric' He even suggests that those reading Christ in the OT are in danger of becoming anti-Semites (RD, 16, 22 Jan. 2020, 14, 15 Febr.).

The Jerusalem of Israel is a concrete, temporary, historically visible and tangible demonstration to the world of God's acts that culminate in Christ. In Israel's Old Testament history, God reveals His grace and His judgments concerning the world and humanity. In it, the name 'Jerusalem' symbolizes everything God has in mind for Israel and for the world. It concerns at least seven geographical and ethnic aspects, respectively: 1.the city, 2.the country, 3.the temple (geographical); and: 4.the people, 5.the kings, 6.the priests, 7.the prophets (ethnic). In all these aspects, Jesus Christ has given to 'Jerusalem' its essential meaning and fulfilment. The city is fulfilled in the new Jerusalem that will descend on the earth (Rev.21); the country is the new creation; the temple is Christ Himself; the people are the communion of believers out of the Jews and the Gentiles of all times and places; the kings, priests and prophets concern the qualities that are united in Christ and realised in all who believe in Him.[59]

The disciples began their mission on behalf of Jesus in Jerusalem with the aim of showing to Jews and Gentiles that all God's Old Testament intentions regarding geographical and ethnic Israel have been gloriously fulfilled in Christ and therefore equally made valid for the whole world and all nations, including the Jewish people.

c. The practical significance

What is the practical significance for our relationship with the present Jewish people if we acknowledge the priority of 'Jerusalem' in the mission of Jesus? First, the words of Jesus make clear that He considers 'Jerusalem' to be part of the mission field. The general order to approach, educate, teach, preach, witness and baptize among all nations precedes the instruction

---

[59] For a careful exegetical interpretation of the fulfilment of Old Testament Israel in Christ, see: Rob Dalrymple, *These Brothers of Mine: A Biblical Theology of Land and Family and a Response to Christian Zionism*, Eugene, Oregon: Wipf & Stock, 2015. [http://www.determinetruth.com/about-me.html] See also: Bram Maljaars, 'And so All Israel will be saved (Rom. 11:26)', in: Paas, *Christian Zionism Examined*, Appendix I.

to begin 'in' or 'at' Jerusalem. The geographical, cultural and historical meaning of 'Jerusalem' does not place geographical and ethnic Israel beyond the focus of the proclaimers of the gospel. If the church wants to obey Jesus' mission, she must therefore also focus her missionary activity on the Jewish people, both inside and outside the present state of Israel, however difficult and laden that may sound.[60]

Unfortunately, it is a reality that the followers of the Jewish (Judaist) religion reject Jesus and His mission. Following many in Western society, the secular, agnostic and atheistic majority of the Jewish people have also turned away from religion in general. Although the church has contributed a lot to the Jewish aversion to Jesus – and this should admonish Christians to be modest – this does not absolve her of her mission. Running away from it out of shame or fear would amount to the worst form of anti-Semitism, namely withholding from the Jews the message of salvation of the world by the Saviour who in His humanity came from their own midst. The black pages of the history of the church do not only pertain to the Jews. Also other peoples have closed their doors to the gospel of Christ because of the bad example of Western Christians of Christ. This sad reality requires much love and tact in designing mission methods and mission plans regarding the hurt and injured and their offspring, who are still living with their traumas.

The disciples had to begin their missionary work in 'Jerusalem'. The question may arise whether 'Jerusalem' should always be the methodical starting point for contemporary missionary activities. In other words, does Jesus want all missionaries and mission organizations anywhere in the world to focus first on work among Jews or in Israel? The answer is negative. Although the disciples are our examples, they also had a unique

---

[60] J. Verkuijl, *Contemporary Missiology*, p. 136-138, acknowledges that the proclamation of the gospel among Jews has often been an internal Jewish matter, but he stresses that Christians from the Gentiles also have a task concerning the Jews: 'Above and beyond this, however, the church needs people whose special training in Judaism equips them for their work of being a bridge to the Jewish people'.

task, which we cannot perform. For specific geographical, cultural and revelation-historical reasons, they had to proclaim in 'Jerusalem' the wonderful fulfilment and realisation in Christ of God's salvation promises to Old Testament Israel. As a result, the history of God's use of Israel as an extraordinary vehicle of His particular revelation has been completed.

In our day the Jewish people, both inside and outside the modern state of Israel, are part of the 'all the world', or 'all nations', from which God elects and gathers His unique people in Christ. Christians who carry the gospel into the world should study in depth the culture and religious situation in which they work. Every missionary is called to a certain people, for some, that is to the Jewish people.

6. Successors of the Sender

a. The apostles

Jesus is the first of all who have been sent. In His great commission, He has shared this position with others. First of all, these are His disciples, then called apostles (*sent ones*). Their initial number of twelve was at some point reduced by Judas, who was replaced by Matthias. The twelve first disciples of Jesus received the great assignment directly from Him. They were very personally engaged by Him and declared participants in His mission. Because of his meeting with Jesus on the way to Damascus, Paul also belongs to them. In the previous chapters, we looked at elements of Jesus' assignment. The apostles had to make a start with the spreading of the gospel to the whole world, including their own birthplace and nation.

On the one hand, the institution of universal mission is completely new. Christ's victory has created a new situation in which He has made the world accessible for the gospel. On the other hand, world mission is a *continuum*, a continuation in new ways of the Old Testament situation, in which the peoples had to pay attention to another number of twelve – namely the 12 tribes of Israel – in order to see a micro-demonstration of God's intentions with the whole world. Israel's functioning as an educational model of God's cosmic plan, however, was temporary, flawed and shadowy. The world did not see much of it. But God's acts with the tribes of Israel culminated in Jesus. For that matter, 'Moses and the prophets' had already foretold this. He became the King of the new Israel, now ethnically and geographically unlimited, embodied in all believers in Christ of all times and places.

In chapter 5 we saw that Jesus wanted the apostles to start in their own environment. But the outpouring of the Holy Spirit on a large international crowd in *Acts* 2 clearly indicated that the beginning of the universal missionary work outside 'Jerusalem' was at hand. However, apparently the apostles still hesitated to involve the pagan peoples in their activity. After all, according to their Jewish tradition these peoples were unclean. The disciples needed further education. Through a miraculous vision in Joppa, the Holy Spirit explained to Peter that he should not regard as unclean what God had declared as clean, and that therefore the non-Jews belong to his mission field (Acts 10 and 11). Later, at the Apostolic Convent in Jerusalem, the last prejudices held by the Jewish preachers of the gospel were removed (Acts 15).

It appeared that Paul, a former Pharisee and a fanatical enemy of the first Christians – who was converted by the intervention of Jesus Himself to become an apostle – immediately openly approached the gentiles with the gospel. In the end, it was the persecutions by the Jewish leaders, the destruction of Jerusalem, the Jewish uprisings, and the removal of many Jews from the country by the Romans, which drove the apostles and the first Jewish Christians beyond Canaan into the world. Jewish opposition against the apostles and their first converts functioned as a means to make their mission universal. Ethnic barriers to their universal mission were further overcome by the blessing and the appearance of Jesus himself (to Paul), by the teaching of the Spirit, and by the political-military conditions in the Roman Empire.

From the outset there was also external opposition against the great commission. The apostles and the first congregations encountered many obstacles and forms of resistance. This often led to life-threatening situations. The first centuries of church history bear witness to a rapid growth of Christianity, but also to bloody persecutions. Many apostles and other Christians died as martyrs.[61] However, it is true that their violent deaths and all the other external attempts of Satan to destroy the church were less dangerous than the ways in which Satan tried to influence the church from within. This writing is not a description of the Christian persecutions and other external dangers that threatened the great commission, but – especially in chapters 7 and 8 – we want to draw the attention to a number

---

[61] 'How did the Apostle die?', https://overviewbible.com/how-did-the-apostles-die/

of internal factors, which are undermining or paralyzing the missionary work in the Western world in our time.

In their succeeding to the prophets of the Old Testament, the apostles were also forerunners. In them the history of all Christians takes shape, and of the history of the entire congregation of Christ, in which they are merged.

b. All Christians

Through the missional words of Jesus, all Christians receive a missionary calling. With those words He identified Himself with and fulfilled the prophetic mission of Israel's calling for the world that went back to the Old Testament. Inspired by the Holy Spirit, the evangelists and the apostles incorporated the missional words of their divinely-sent Master into the Scriptures. The first Christians took over the task of 'educating' or 'teaching'. This does not mean that they carried out about their task in a traditional classroom situation. For the first Christians, mission was much more than teaching or learning in a narrow sense. They committed themselves to it with the whole of their lives, in words and deeds. Flemming shows from the New Testament how missionary patterns and methods developed among the first Christians to bring the gospel message close to the people in their pagan context.[62]

Through the ages, Christians have followed the example of the apostles and the first Christians. They have spread the gospel in the world, nearby and in distant regions, among their own relatives, in their own family and beyond, in depth and breadth. Like the apostles and the first Christians, they have always had many problems to overcome. In general, there has always been opposition from the outside, from the world where Satan still has his domain. Harsh violence and cunning subversion alternated, trying to silence Christians. Often, Christians were better resistant to harsh persecutions than to the soft hand of deception and seduction. Courage, willingness to sacrifice and missionary attitude when facing oppression and contempt,

---

[62] Dean Flemming, *Contextualization in the New Testament: Patterns for Theology and Mission*, Intervarsity, 2005.

often characterizes Christians in countries where freedom has been restricted by hostile powers. In such a context the call for obedience to the great commission is at the same time a challenge to confess one's choice: either being of Christ, or being against Him. In free countries without persecution, the choices are more subtle. But the challenge for Christians remains, to be a missionary of Christ in all circumstances.

c. The congregation

All individual Christians have been sent on mission into the world by Christ. Likewise, the *congregation* or the *church* as an organism has been sent by Him too. To me the two terms are not really different, but in this booklet I mainly use the first name, because it more clearly expresses the local appearance of the community of Christians. Many have written about the congregation and her mission. Michael Goheen[63] explained the missionary identity of the congregation (church) by looking at the role which believers play throughout Scripture. For both, congregation and believers, Van 't Hof is right in claiming: We have been sent in Him [Christ]. In Him, we participate in mission. Only in Him our mission organization can be sent to those who are outside Him.[64]

The mission of the congregation rests on the New Testament apostles, who, as disciples of Christ, fulfilled the mission of Old Testament Israel and the prophets. The *Creed of Nicea*, therefore, calls the church 'apostolic'. Christians cannot live without communion with Christ and fellow believers. Christians are members of each other and of Christ. Together they are the 'Body of Christ' (1 Cor.12:27; Eph.5:23), or, as the *Apostolic Creed* says, 'the communion of saints'. This defines

---

[63] Micheal W. Goheen, *A Light to the Nations: The Missional Church and the Biblical Story*, Baker Academic, 2011.

[64] However, I.P.C. van 't Hof, *Het zendingsbegrip van Karl Barth*, Hoenderloo: Zendingsstudieraad, 1946, p.119, 120, creates a contradiction by asserting that the church, whereas rooted in Christ, is not the goal and cause of the reality of mission. He is not right because the church is the Body of Christ, who is both the Sender and the One who has been sent.

the congregation or the church as a missionary organism, either locally or universally. Here, I leave undiscussed that different church denominations have emerged over time, each of which claims the title 'communion of saints'. For the problem of ecclesiastical divisions, see chapter 9, section e

Church history shows two realities of the relationship between the congregation and the world. First of all, it cannot be denied that usually the world has not warmly welcomed the congregation. There has not been any period in history without persecutions of the church in parts of the world. That is also true for now. [65]

The second fact that should be stressed is that the congregation has very often been unfaithful to her identity, by mixing with the powers of the world that have been working against God and His kingdom. Persecution is not always caused by the world, but sometimes also by the attitude of Christians. In chapter 2, section c, we described some examples of 'Christian' acts that have provoked negative reactions. Particularly as European Christians, we must admit that Christianity often was on the side of the persecutors. In much of the world, the church has been pulling the strings for over a thousand years and making very dirty hands. Christians in Europe more often were persecutors instead of being persecuted. As a result, the identity of the congregation as being sent by Christ has weakened or has become unrecognizable. In any case, mixing with the world of political and economic powers has harmed the apostolic nature of individual Christians and of the congregation of Christians.

My American co-reader Mark Thiesen at this point refers to the situation in the USA, where the name of Christians has been sullied by their involvement in politics in their campaign against abortion, homosexual rights, and some other things at the national level. They formed an organization called 'Moral Majority'and had much influence, especially in the 1980s, in influencing legislation, and they had the ear of some

[65] The Open Doors ranking list of persecutions of Christians (2020) includes 50 countries. In 11 countries the persecutions are 'extreme', in 34 countries 'very heavy', and in 5 countries 'heavy'. See: opendoors.nl/ranglijst

powerful people like Presidents Reagan and even Trump. Although Thiesen agrees with their concerns, he observes that their use of power to achieve their aims has left a bitter taste in other peoples' mouths, which helped to stereotype Christians as being intolerant and power-hungry.

If the church or the congregation is mixed with political and economic powers, this immediately affects the other side of the missionary medal. After all, the congregation has not only been sent, but it is also a sender herself. Actually, the history of the church can be described as a history of mission. The congregation is essentially a missionary institution. However, a congregation that gradually allows worldly influences to determine her identity is in the process of losing her nature as a missionary community. It is important to stop that shocking process. In order to do that, we need the redeeming power of Jesus. But first, the characteristics of this loss of missionary identity must be envisioned. Let us look at some examples in the following two chapters.

7. (Un)limited atonement

a. 'Jesus did not die for everyone'

For some Christians, consciously or unconsciously, this phrase in the title functions as a reason for not really committing themselves to the spreading of the gospel to their neighbours nearby or far away. There are few Christians, though, who would like to deny the global significance of the work of Jesus. After all, God loves the world, and therefore He sent His Son, so that all who believe in Him are saved. At the Second Coming, this great cosmic salvific event will culminate in the creation of a new heaven and a new earth. Almost all Christians agree that the advent of Jesus to world and humanity is of universal and general interest.

But there is less agreement when it comes to the meaning of His suffering and death on the cross, where He shed His blood for the forgiveness or the atonement of the sins of individuals. 'Whom did Jesus die for?' Once I was asked that question during a job interview at a Christian school. The conversation went promisingly, until my open-minded answer to that question: 'For everyone of course!' Are you right in saying to your neighbours and others who do not know Christ that His sin-atoning work is valid for every human being? From then onward I have realised that a considerable number of Christians are answering this question negatively. They think that making Jesus' atoning death generally valid goes against an important biblical truth. According to them such a generalisation would jeopardize the recognition of the free will and sovereign choice of God. Some Christians conclude from the sovereignty of God that the blood of Jesus has not been shed for the atonement of the sins of every human being. Yet remarkably, these Christians would generously recognize that the blood of Jesus is 'more than sufficient' to atone for the sins of all men. They then point to a certain phrase in the *Canons of Dort*, an influential confessional document from the time just after the 16th-century Reformation.[66] But they do not agree to the view that, in a certain way, the shedding of the blood of Jesus is valid for every human being. Such a thought they consider to be the error of 'general atonement' or 'general reconciliation'. Strikingly, for this rejection they refer to the same *Canons of Dort*.[67]

It is meant that Jesus, with His suffering and dying on Calvary, has only effectively reconciled or saved those people who believe in Him, and who turn out to have been chosen by God. The blood of Jesus is considered too precious to have also been shed for those who have remained disbelievers.

b. Legitimate concern

Is it right to appeal to the *Canons of Dort* and the *TULIP* summary of 'calvinism' in order to reject any universal significance of Christ's atoning work? I do not think that is the case. However, in saying so, I do not disparage the thought that the blood of Jesus on the one hand is sufficient for all and on the other hand effective for the elect only. It is not just an ingenuity formulated by hobby theologians. In fact, that view is quite understandable when one considers that the doctrine of 'limited atonement' is motivated by a serious concern about the human tendency not to allow God be truly God. The defenders of this doctrine rightly stress that faith in Christ, which saves from eternal loss, is not a product of the free or autonomous choice of man, but of the sovereign choice of God, who, with His eter-

---

[66] By the *Canons of Dort* (1618-1619) the reformed Christians of The Netherlands in five articles opposed the Remonstrants or Arminians. Article II, 3, under the heading 'The Infinite Value of Christ's Death', says: 'This death of God's Son is the only and entirely complete sacrifice and satisfaction for sins; it is of infinite value and worth, more than sufficient to atone for the sins of the whole world.'. https://www.apuritansmind.com/creeds-and-confessions/the-synod-of-dordt-1618-1619-a-d/

[67] *Canons of Dort*, Article II,8: 'In other words, it was God's will that Christ through the blood of the cross (by which he confirmed the new covenant) should effectively redeem from every people, tribe, nation, and language all those and only those who were chosen from eternity to salvation and given to him by the Father'.

nal Fatherly arms, forms the solid foundation of the salvation of His children. Faith is God's gift (Eph.2:1-10).

Ultimately, only that final fact assures Christians of their being rescued from sin and death. After all, if the salvation of Christians rested on their own thoughts or emotions, then it would have an extremely shaky basis. Faith is firm and unshakeable because God is its source, although believers in themselves are often very weak and doubting. They find their assurance in Him, not in themselves. Their 'names are written in heaven' (Lk.10:20), because He' engraved 'them 'on the palms of His hands' (Is.49:14-16).

There is another serious reason for the assertion of limited reconciliation. Its defenders say that if Jesus' atoning blood had been shed for all, then all human beings of all times and places would have been redeemed, to be finally saved. In this sense, the concept of 'general reconciliation' would be the cause of an even more serious error, namely that of 'universal reconciliation'

It is good to realise that the background of the view that Christ's atoning work is limited may have been motivated by the desire to defend biblical core truths in reverence for God. It is important to recognize God's sovereignty and election, and also to emphasize the need to receive personally from God the gifts of rebirth, faith, and repentance together with justification and sanctification. When it comes to the saving effect of the blood of Jesus in particular persons, there is indeed no general reconciliation. However, we must remember that a 'limitation', thus conceived, does not only concern the atoning work of Jesus, but all His acts of salvation. The redemptive effect of the entire work of Jesus is limited to people who believe in Him.

c. Not everyone will be saved

The sad truth that salvation does not include everyone underlines the serious objection against the concept of universal reconciliation. It is simply not true that ultimately everyone will be saved. We are facing the awesome and unfathomable realities of sin, death and loss, in which unfortunately many remain trapped. In the final analysis, natural man appears to prefer being caught in a life without God than to choose a life with God.

Christians do not surrender to that dark reality. We know our God-given responsibility, and flee to Jesus who delivers us, and we encourage others to do the same. We assure ourselves and others that from God's side there is nothing to prevent us from seeking refuge with our Saviour. That is precisely why and how Christians participate in the mission of Jesus in accordance with His great commission. But at the same time, we entirely depend on God's electing omnipotence, which does not include salvation for all. So there is the sad reality that not everyone will be saved. Apart from God's grace and the saving atonement in Christ, there are the realities of Satan, hell, and judgment. Neglecting those notions is a serious matter. It makes the message of salvation for lost people implausible and ultimately meaningless. Faith in Jesus is decisive for the future of all men and women: either eternal happiness with Him or eternal loss without Him. God is eager to give that saving faith to anyone who resorts to Jesus in the needs of his or her life.

d. Unlimited grace

Do the erroneous teachings of 'general reconciliation' and 'universal reconciliation' for all result from too broad a view of the work of Jesus? Some sincere Christians emphatically say so. Their argument seems to be justified by the widespread superficial or cheap visions of Jesus among nominal Christians that have the tendency to only advance secularization further. In support of their conviction of limited atonement, they refer to various Bible texts. However, the seemingly opposing view of unlimited reconciliation is no less supported by Scripture.[68]

---

[68] Cf. a consideration of Bible portions quoted by adherents of the contradicting views of general atonement, limited atonement, and universal atonement: Daniel R. Hyde, 'For whom did Jesus die?', https://tabletalkmagazine.com/posts/for-whom-did-christ-die/; 'Whom did Jesus die for?', https://www.gotquestions.org/who-did-Jesus-die-for.html; 'Voor wie is Christus gestorven?' http://www.internetbijbelschool.nl/htmldoc/voorwiegestorven.htm .

I think that these errors are not necessarily linked to an unbiblically broad understanding of the work of Jesus. The greatness and multi-sidedness of Jesus' work cannot be overestimated. That is precisely why one cannot separate the shedding of His atoning blood on Calvary – as something specific to certain people – from the all-encompassing meaning of the fact that He has been sent by the Father as Saviour of the world and humanity. His cosmic acts of salvation concern the whole of Christmas, Good Friday, Easter, Ascension, Pentecost and the Second Coming. With His suffering, death, and resurrection, He acquired God's true offer of atonement and salvation to all. He paved the way, so that everyone could be reconciled with God.

In that sense, the validity of His atonement and redemption and the scope of its offer to humanity are unlimited. God's love and grace have no limits in Christ. No one should feel left out. Not any category of people can apologize afterwards by saying that the gospel of reconciliation did not apply to them.

The message of the entire gospel, including the tidings of His atoning work, is destined for all. That is precisely why the act of rejecting Jesus by many is such a serious matter. For they look down on the loving offer of God. They are not interested in the atonement of their sins and the sacrifice Jesus made for them. He came and died for everyone, but unfortunately not everyone has accepted Him.

Here we respect the mystery of election by God in Christ of *not-all*, and His offer of reconciliation in Christ *to all*. What God does and what He expects from our responsibility cannot be forced into a rational system, which would make everything comprehensible to us. After all, He is infinitely great and we are small limited creatures. He is the omniscient, we are not. Faith accepts that mystery.

e. Consequences for mission

What are the consequences of the (sometimes seemingly) opposing views of atonement for obeying the great commission of Jesus? Of course, Christians are encouraged to partake in mission by the open-minded view that the atoning work of Jesus should be offered to all because He died for all. However, the described notion that Jesus would not have died for all men weakens the urgency of mission, including the proclamation of reconciliation. That may be one of the reasons why the missionary work by Western Christians did not really get underway before the 19th century and by some only in the 20th century. But today, fortunately, this view seems to be no longer blocking missionary activities by many of its supporters. We would like to acknowledge that there are many examples of flourishing missionary work by Christians who, at least in theory, believe in the doctrine of limited atonement.

But there is also the other side, especially among those who think schematically, and who rationalistically draw extreme consequences from the doctrine of limited atonement. After all, if in our vision the atoning work of Jesus does not apply to everyone, then we may be guided by the idea that God's election necessarily limits the work of Jesus to certain people. This can easily lead to the conclusion that His work may not be destined for 'our neighbours'. If Jesus has been sent to the world by God the Father, but not for everyone, the people whom we meet or most of them, may be excluded. It is obvious that the Christians who follow this line of reasoning and therefore consistently apply the law of logic, can lean towards the opinion that mission does not (much) matter. If it is not certain whether the gospel of God's salvation is meant for your neighbours or for your potential audiences, why put time and effort into attempts to convert them? Moreover, if they are chosen, they will eventually get to reconciliation and salvation anyway, even without your commitment.

Obviously, this logic, if applied in its extreme consequence, first of all contradicts the nucleus of the gospel, as for example expressed by Jesus through the Apostle John (John.3:16).[69] Furthermore, it makes sincere Christians doubt

---

[69] Cf. 'for the world/ all/ all people/ everybody': John 1:29, 3:15-19; Acts10:43; Rom.5:18; 2 Cor.5:14,15,19; 1 Tim.2:1-6, 4:10; Titus 2:11; Hebr.2:9; 2 Petr. 2:1,9, 3:9; 1 John 2:2.

their own election and salvation. Subsequently, it undermines the motivation to participate, personally and ecclesiastically, in the mission of Jesus in the world. For that matter, why should people who do not believe in Christ be interested in a a message about atonement by Christ, who after all may not have died for them? Ultimately, this view can be used as an excuse for the ambivalence of calling oneself a Christian and at the same time not functioning as a missionary Christian in the world. In the next chapter we look at more examples of escape behaviour among Christians.

8. Evasions

a. Dodging behaviour

What about the obedience of Christians to the great commission of Jesus? Let us look at our own environment, the countries of Western culture. The practical situation in the modern West shows that complying with Jesus' great commission is by no means something that we can take for granted. Nominal Christians try to make the impression that they are Christians. But if the relationship with Christ has no depth or is actually absent, they are not touched by loving and urgent incentives to be witnesses to Christ, at home, at work, or at school. That is because they have a consumer mentality regarding the love of God and the grace of Christ, ultimately possessing a faith without real meaning.

But also truly-believing Christians, who are inwardly connected to Christ, are sometimes consciously or unconsciously inclined to shy away from the challenge to radiate in words and deeds to their surroundings the love and grace of the tri-une God. Sometimes they are members of churches or congregations that are not interested in missionary work or do not give it priority. The dodging of the task of mission occurs in many ways and gradations. Let us look at some forms of evasion among Christians.

b. 'It is work for specialists and the rich'

It is quite common among Western Christians not to make themselves available for mission and not give (material) support to others who have volunteered to do so in their environment. They think that mission either in their own environment or far away is a responsibility for specialists and wealthy Christians. They believe that they themselves do not have sufficient knowledge and financial capacity for this. Poverty as an excuse to get rid of missionary work, one would expect in the 'third' world, but the growing gap between the rich and the poor also plays a role in the West. However, excusing oneself because of intellectual inability and (relative) poverty cannot stand. All Christians have received gifts (1 Cor.12). The apostles and first Christians were very simple and poor people. They made the church grow. And over the centuries, it has been the simple and those with limited means who have made the church grow.

c. 'The work is unnecessary'

Among philosophically oriented Christians, the necessity of missionary activity is increasingly doubted. Many believe that winning people for Christ is not necessary. Jesus and the apostles lived a long time ago. In the meantime, we have discovered that eventually all people will be saved, regardless of their religion or theology. All people, including Jews (Judaists), Muslims, Buddhists, adherents of natural religions, and animists, have each their own way to the same God. Even agnostics and atheists will eventually find their way to God. Christians who shun worship meetings because they are only nominal members will also be saved. Churches that have mixed the authority of the gospel of Christ with salvific expectations of non-biblical thought systems or religions are also finding their way to God and to salvation. In general, adherents of this liberal view of 'reconciliation for all' trust that in the end all people who, like themselves, lead a 'good' life will be saved. Consequently, they think that mission is a futile effort, not worth spending energy and money on.

We wonder to which extent this idea of religious pluralism – that one religion is as good as another and all beliefs are valid – has even affected traditionally church-going Christians. Deep down many may doubt that others are lost. To imply that Jesus is the only Saviour seems bigoted. So many of us are happy to let others find their own way to heaven. The effect is the same. They don't share their faith.

The answer to this evasion can be short. People who adhere to this view, contradict Jesus. After all, He says about Himself: 'I am the Way, the Truth and the Life. No-one comes to the Father except through Me' (John 14:6). In chapter 4, section b we discussed this text. Despite grateful recognition of the remaining good points in all kinds of religions and worldviews, we must stress that God does not present to us any other way of salvation than the one in which we surrender to Jesus Christ and focus our faith solely on Him. There is simply no other way. That is not to say that non-biblical religions and thought systems cannot contain elements of truth. The point is that those elements of truth in themselves do not redeem or save man. They sometimes constitute good tools for making the gospel land.[70]

A connected problem is that many Western Christians no longer believe in hell, that a loving God would send people there. This comes from our society's increasing inability to understand the seriousness of sin and guilt. If sin were not so terrible, Jesus would not have died on the cross. But we tend to whitewash sin today. Then we don't realize that each sin is like driving another nail into the Lord, which makes us guilty. Only if there were no real guilt, there would not be a need for hell.

Apart from the liberal version of the doctrine of recon-ciliation for all, it must be acknowledged that certainly not all people who believe some form of this idea necessarily reject mission. For example, Karl Barth seems to say that basically everyone has been saved, but that not everyone knows it. That is why this news has to be announced to them. Another exam-ple concerns the well-known missionary Johann Krapf. He was an adherent of the so-called *Hahn'sche Gemeinschaft* in Würt-temberg, and of the conviction that unbelievers will also be saved, although, after they have suffered a (very long) period in hell.[71] Related to that is the thought that many will be saved by Christ, without having known Him as Jesus or without having heard of Him. I recognize the serious mental struggle about the awesome problem of the eternal destiny of those who could not know Jesus. Yet in the Bible I find no basis for the idea of an ultimate reconciliation for all and I think that we should leave

---

[70] This we have discussed in chapter 4, section e.

[71] See a discussion on Krapf's involvement in this sect, in my: *Johannes Rebmann: A Servant of God in Africa Before the Rise of Western Colonial-ism*, Bonn: VKW, 2018, p.28-30, 34, 35,68, 253-256.

this impenetrable secret in the hands God (Dt.29:29). At the same time, we want to respect Paul's warning in *Romans* 1:20, which we discussed in chapter 4, section e.

d. 'We are not (yet) good enough for it'

Perhaps this evasion is the most dangerous one, because seemingly strong motives are used. Some Christians say or think they cannot perform mission because they are not or not yet good enough for it. Our congregation is so weak. We do not have much youth. We are not well organized yet, because we are missing good leaders. There are so many apostates among us and there are so many sins. Many of us do not know enough about the Bible and of Christian doctrines. We do not have members who could be missionaries or evangelists. First, let us try to solve these problems. Let us first train or be trained as disciples, then we can go out for mission and show that we are good Christians. First, let us try to become stronger, healthier and more religious. We are not capable of it yet. But in the future, if we have become good enough, then we will start to be a missionary minded congregation.

This objection is defended with pious arguments at first sight. It is true that, as Christians, we must realize, and confess our weaknesses and sins, and that we must fight them. But can we excuse our disobedience to Christ, by referring to these weaknesses? On second thoughts, the argumentation is misleading. First of all, because it is assumed that we can be good enough for Christ's mission if we did our best first. Moreover, it is tacitly assumed that we would be able to lay the foundation of a healthy and well-organized church and a holier personal life, and then – after we have laid this foundation – God could continue to build on what we have achieved. The idea means that we must prepare before God can do His work in and with us. Only when we are ready can God come to use us as missionaries and evangelists.

However, this way of reasoning certainly goes against Scripture. Be assured that it does not belong to Christians. It is a line of thought that shows a lack of knowledge of Christ and

His work. After all, a congregation or church continues to be called for mission, even though she is unhealthy, not well organized and weak. The same goes for individual men and women who are Christians. We are called to testify to Christ, although our knowledge and behaviour are not perfect. A congregation will never be perfect. Nor will a Christian ever achieve perfection in this world. But although congregations and Christians are not perfect, they are challenged throughout the world to obey the great commission. For our 'power is made perfect in weakness' (2 Cor.12:7-10). Sometimes our own imperfections if they are freely confessed can make us more real in the eyes of outsiders. If they see that we are truly human but are still trying, they may come to see that the gospel is for ordinary people too, not just super-saints. Our honesty in this area about our own failures helps combat the stereotype that all Christians are hypocrites. The Spirit of Christ uses imperfect people.

Just look at the Christians of Corinth. Paul calls them 'sanctified in Christ' and 'called to be holy' (1 Cor.1:2). He awakens them to be missionary examples, to win others for Christ. But in the same epistle, he admonishes them for many weaknesses and sins. In the congregation there were divisions and quarrels (1:10-17; 3:1-4), unspiritual behaviour (3:1-2), pride (4:6-16), immorality (5:1-4), engaging secular judges in conflicts among brethren (6:1-8), abusing the Lord's Supper, drunkenness (11:17-22), disorderly worship (14:26-40), doubting the resurrection from the dead (5:12), and some had no idea of who God is (3:34). The Christians of Corinth were therefore far from perfect. Yet they were called by Paul 'church of God' and 'sanctified in Christ' (1:1,2). Despite everything, the Christians of Corinth were a sacred community. In their ancient Greek world, they were called to apply Christ's message to themselves, and to carry it into their environment. They did not receive that calling because of their own immaculate behaviour or their strong faith, but because of the grace of God.

The men and women of the congregation of Corinth were holy and called for mission because of the work Christ had done on the cross of Calvary. Through that work, they were able to approach the surrounding world with the liberating message of forgiveness of sins and peace with God, and to let the world know about the promise of eternal life by Christ for all who believe in Him. Their imperfection and flaws made it necessary for the Christians in Corinth to seek the grace of Christ daily, in order to receive from Him forgiveness, sanctification and missionary direction. Christ was their strength. They were no exception to the universal reality of humanity's need for Him as the Saviour.

e. 'You cannot impose it on them'

Adding urgency to the great commission, like Jesus Himself did, is not popular. Today it is apt to be linked to the time when in the West Christianity was still widely accepted and influential. Then, political powers and social control made it virtually impossible to ignore the congregation and the Christian culture. History offers numerous examples of forced conversions. They are shallow and do not reach beyond a certain cultural adaptation. Apparently, Christianity in the West for centuries has been not much more than a thin varnish. Now, the process of secularization has removed Christianity from the centres of power and public influence. This marks the end of any form of coerced conversion. There is freedom of religion. Imposing your faith on anyone is impossible and forbidden. Acknowledging that truth is a good thing, and has been generally accepted in the Western world.

But there is also another aspect to it. Christians have sometimes become hesitant concerning the great mission of Jesus. Does not openly witnessing His Name create enmity in secular society, because it reminds people of past Christian coercion? Isn't it inappropriate or intrusive to proclaim the gospel in a secularized context? Surely, we can't push our religious standard down their throats, can we?

However, these hesitations are unnecessary. Because, partly due to the secularization, among Christians more room has been created for a spiritual vision of the great commission of Jesus. His message is urgent, indeed. But He does not force people with earthly power, because His kingdom is not of this world. This most important lesson the apostles and after them all Christians have had to learn. The love of Christ urges those who have been sent by Him to let fellow human beings know about their Saviour who died and was resurrected in their place (2 Cor.5:14). Being sent out 'like lambs among the wolves'(Lk.10:3), they are guided by the Spirit of the meek, who will 'inherit the earth' (Mt.5:5). The same Spirit convinces people that they have broken God's law and are lost as sinners if they do not flee to Christ for salvation (Gal.3:19-26). Jesus intends Christians to spread this message boldly in words and deeds, even if the target group is less than easy. That is not an act of haughty compulsion or arrogant condescension, but the attitude of a friendly guide who shows the right way.

f. 'I don't like it'

We conclude our list of evasions by referring to the problem of apathy. The word is derived from the Greek *apatheia*, resignation or insensibility. In people who are caught by this problem, there is a lack of emotion, motivation and/or enthusiasm. Apathetic people are lethargic and indifferent; they do not show empathy and have adopted a passive attitude. They don't feel like getting engaged in anything. This is not about the phenomenon of apatheism or apathyism, terms that indicate a modern form of practical atheism.[72]

But now we are discussing the problem of passive Christians. Often, this concerns form Christians or nominal Christians, who suffer from spiritual apathy. This is about 'comfortable Christianity', people who may come to church but never volunteer for anything or get involved beyond attendance. They feel 'safe' doing the bare minimum; so that is enough for them. It is a kind of 'minimalist Christianity', which

---

[72]Wikipedia https://en.wikipedia.org/wiki/Apatheism) : 'Apatheists may feel that even if there were a god/deity and the existence and legitimacy of them were proven, it would not make a difference to them for one reason or another, therefore, which one(s), if any, are real does not matter and any discussion about it is meaningless'.

is tied to a legalistic understanding of the faith. God expects me to do the things on this list, and if I fulfill those requirements I'm on the safe side.

The fact that there is no alternative way to salvation does not affect passive Christians. The truth that outside Christ all the roads are dead ends, does not seem to touch them. It does not affect them for their own situation. In any case, this awesome reality does not move them with regard to the destination of others. They are indifferent to the fate of unbelievers. This phenomenon is a serious problem, for three interrelated reasons.

First of all it is a problem for the apathetic members of the congregation themselves, because Christ does not really mean anything to them. and therefore they are in danger of getting lost. It is also a problem for the congregation, because it threatens her identity as a communion of Christ. Their apathetic attitude is primarily a problem because it jeopardizes participation in the mission of Jesus to the world.

9. Hindrances

a. A horizontal dividing line

The previous chapter was about evasive attitudes of individual (nominal) Christians, that stand in the way of their participation in mission. This chapter deals with possible weaknesses in the congregation, her structure and culture, which hinder participation in the mission of Jesus Christ.

We first consider the way in which the leadership in the congregation is dealt with. In *Hebrews* 13:7,17 (cf. 1 Thess.5:12,13) Christians are admonished to remember their 'leaders' because of their work, to 'submit to their authority', and to recognize that they watch over their souls.

In some ecclesiastical traditions, from the era of Antiquity onward, these and other texts have been abused to justify a strict hierarchy in the church, a horizontal separation between believers. The bishops, the preachers or pastors/ reverends with the elders in their councils hold 'special posts' and are above the dividing line. The rest of the Christians in the congregation have a place underneath, in the position of 'lay-people', or 'the office of all believers'. The making of decisions is reserved for the officials above the dividing line. They are supposed to have received their calling 'from Above' and represent Christ. The other Christians do not have that special connection. They are in a position where they are 'below' or 'opposite' the leaders of the congregation.

However, this structure undermines the organic character of the congregation and weakens her missionary nature, which reminds *all* men and women in the congregation that they have been sent into the world. After all, the being-called out of the world and the being-sent to the world, originates in the salvation initiative of God through the *Missio Dei*, and determines the structure of the church. This means that the congregation basically consist of two levels, firstly her Head, Christ, and secondly, under Him, the believers. The believers are connected to Christ and to each other. In one Body, with

Him as the Head,[73] all believers have their place, task, function and responsibility, according to the talents and vocation God has given to each person. The variety of contributions of all believers can be summarized as a multitude of ministries.

The image of the body illustrates that these ministries of the members can be very different. But all members are subordinate to and connected to the Head. That order is the only form of hierarchy in the church. Therefore, all share in the kingship, priesthood and prophet role of Christ.[74] Moreover, all receive their gifts from the Holy Spirit, although different gifts.[75] The relationship with Christ and the Holy Spirit puts the differences between the ministries in perspective and indicates that one member of the Body is not above another and that one member cannot function without another. All Christians have a certain responsibility for preaching, pastorate, diaconate, and mission.

We gratefully recognize that some Christians have received special gifts for these tasks. But they do not, therefore, represent the top of an authoritarian pyramid. Through their examples, they serve the congregation to be a missionary community and they help their fellow members to be witnesses of Christ. Their stimulating, equipping, and regulatory tasks prevent Christians from acting individually, apart from the congregation with its many gifts (1 Cor.12), and from getting disconnected from their Sender, Christ.

b. A vertical dividing line

The missionary characteristic of the congregation and her members can also be damaged by the assumption of an invisible vertical separation, which divides the affiliated members into believers and unbelievers. The idea has been formed that both categories are to be considered as legal members of the

---

[73] Eph.5:23. See: *Confessio Belgica*, article 28. The indication 'priesthood of all believers' has a disadvantage, because it does not express the kingship and prophetship of all believers.

[74] 1 Petr.2:9; Rev.1:6; cf. Ex.19:6.

[75] 1 Cor.12.

congregation. However, the Body of Christ cannot possibly be connected to people who are registered as members of the congregation, but do not believe in Him. By definition, the congregation of Christ consists of believers. It is very important to maintain this truth in the missionary situation of the congregation. When calling the unbelievers in the surrounding world to repent, to convert, and to become members of the Body, the congregation would lose all credibility if it allowed non-believers to be legitimate members. In asserting this, we recognize that not any believer has a perfect faith and that ultimately only God can determine who does and who does not belong to His church.

The principle of the incongruity of a vertical separation in the congregation is not generally accepted. Some appeal to Augustine, the church father, who in his fight against the radical Donatists called the congregation a 'corpus permixtum', a 'mixed body'.[76] Calvin, in his opposition to the Anabaptist radicals, agreed to Augustine regarding this issue.[77] They meant first and foremost that the church on earth and her believing members are not perfect. In the congregation, members having a weak faith are mixed with members having a strong faith. New believers have their place as well as those who have advanced on the way of faith. With all of us, faith is imperfect. We need the vicarious work of Christ on a daily basis in order to be justified and sanctified before God. By His grace Christ is making up for our individual and corporate failings. Although the congregation originates from above, in her earthly appearance she has all the characteristics of human work, and therefore she is flawed and incomplete. In her weakness, the congregation on earth, daily needs to realise how dependent she is on the perfect righteousness and holiness of Christ, her Head.

---

[76] W.C.H. Frend, *The Donatist Church: A Movement of Protest in Roman Northern Africa*, Oxford University Press, 1985[2], p. 205, 206; cf. Steven Paas, *A Conflict on Authority in the Early African Church: Augustine of Hippo and the Donatists*, Zomba: Kachere, 2005.

[77] Calvin, *Institutes*, IV: I,8,9,13,17; VIII,12.

Augustine and Calvin, therefore, do not assume a legal vertical separation in the congregation. By the 'mixed character' of the church on earth, they mean that among those who belong to the appearance of the church, not everyone has come to faith in Christ. This does not concern people from outside the congregation who show an interest in her meetings or education. In the church in Antiquity, that category was referred to as *catechumens*; today we might sometimes call them *alpha students*. Hopefully, they will come to personal faith, and therefore are in a stage of preparation for formal affiliation with the congregation. For the time being, however, they are not yet considered as members of the congregation.

The mixed composition of the congregation, referred to by Augustine and Calvin, does not pertain to the normal situation that with her there are the small children of the believers, who have not yet been able to make a conscious choice of faith. After all, by baptizing or dedicating infants, the congregation shows that they belong to her in one way or another. Despite differences in baptismal views, Christians acknowledge that God does not allow to any citizen of the world the option of remaining an unbeliever. After all, God 'wants all men to be saved and to come to a knowledge of the truth'.[78] This emphatic desire of God applies to all people outside the church and to all people within the church. Therefore, He does not allow the (baptized) children in the congregation the liberty of being or remaining unbelievers. They are included in the community of the congregation and bear the responsibility of deliberately taking a decision concerning God's call to personal faith.

However, God does not force them. There is the reality that many have preferred to be or to remain in the position of unbelievers. Unfortunately, there is a possibility that they will not make that choice of faith because they do not want to belong to Christ. In refusing to accept Christ in personal faith, they put themselves outside the congregation. Outwardly, however, this does not always appear, because, although they are

---

[78] 1 Tim.2:3,4.

unbelievers, they sometimes, for all sorts of reasons, remain affiliated with the congregation as a visible institution.

Here it becomes clear why the term 'mixed', is used for the congregation. We cannot deny the fact that being-mixed is a reality in the existence of the congregation in its appearance as a man-made organisation. Not all who formally belong to the institute are also living members of the Body of Christ. Those who lack true faith are nominal Christians. Essentially, they are outside the congregation as an organism. By her very nature, the congregation does not have a department for people who are not members of Christ. Unbelievers do not belong to her and, therefore, they are not legitimate members. Sometimes, it is easy to distinguish them from the believers, if they do not hide their rebellion against God and live in sin openly. Then, the congregation has to admonish them lovingly, but ultimately also she has to take their membership of the institute from them, if they continue to disobey admonitions and refuse to change their wicked lives.

More difficult is the situation regarding those who pretend to be believers, although in their hearts they refuse to surrender to Christ in faith. Often, for a long time, they cannot be distinguished from sincere believers. Article 29, the *Confessio Belgica* refers to them as *hypocrites*, who are mixed among the true members while they do not belong to Christ. The congregation is not called to detect these hidden hypocrites through censure and excommunication. That would be simply impossible, for only God knows the hearts. Jesus warns against attempts to do so in the parable of the weeds between wheat.[79] The falseness of their faith often only appears in situations of trial, which challenge them to make an unconditional choice of faith. In the crises of life members show whether they are believers or not.

Not all unbelieving 'Christians' are aware of their hypocrisy. It is precisely the confrontation with the Word of God, for example in the preaching of gospel or in the testimony of a

---

[79] Mt.13:24-30.

brother or sister, which may help hypocrites to discover who they are and lead them to repentance and conversion. An example is Nicodemus, who during his nightly meeting with Jesus found out that he was not a true believer because he had not yet been born again (John 3:1-21). Nicodemus was in the state of self-deception (1 Cor. 4:4). When we are in such a condition it is impossible for us to be freed without intervention of the Holy Spirit. True believers have been born from the Holy Spirit, who applies to them the justifying and sanctifying work of Christ. This activity of the Holy Spirit in her members visualizes the heavenly origin of the congregation as the Body of Christ.[80] Only in that capacity, without a supposed vertical separation within her, can the congregation really be a missionary congregation.

c. Inequality

An ecclesiastical climate in which members look down on each other is harmful to her participation in the great mission of Jesus. The missionary effectiveness of the congregation is linked to the recognition that her members are equal. This does not deny that there are considerable differences between Christians. But that fact does not diminish their equality in value. The church finds her strength in the connection with Christ. She is a living organism associated with Him. She functions with equal members, who all have received from Christ through the Holy Spirit their own talent(s) and personal callings. In order to be able to approach the world convincingly and successfully with the gospel, the congregation needs every member.

Some think that mission is primarily a task of prominent, intellectual and theologically trained men. In the light of the Bible this view has proved to be unfounded. World and humanity are complex with endless variations. There is great difference in focus between the antennas of people. The number of the points of contact[81] for connecting the gospel is great,

---

[80] Joh.3:3-7.

[81] See chapter 4, sections c, de, and e.

and in their nature they are very different from each other. Consequently, not any Christian in the congregation, however competent or pious, can reach every one of them. This means that every unbeliever in the world needs a certain Christian, who is particularly gifted to make him or her receive and understand the message of Jesus. Whereas some Christian collides with a wall of rejection, another Christian gets access to the heart of the unbeliever.

In today's world the priests, minister and pastors, who in theory are the most qualified to share the message because of their training and experience, may often be the least effective in reaching the lost, because people are suspicious of the clergy. They are more likely to trust the people that they know on a personal basis at work or in their neighbourhood. If the 'ordinary' Christians of the congregation don't participate in mission, then our communities will not be reached. No Christian should be overlooked in the mission of Jesus.

d. Apartheid

The great commission of Jesus is directed at all peoples. God has no racial or ethnic preferences. Christ works supranationally. For the gospel, all nations are of equal value. Without full-heartedly recognizing this equality, congregations would be unable to participate in mission anytime, anywhere.[82]

In chapter 2, section c, we saw that the church in the context of Western culture has often been guilty of cooperation with violent powers that subjected, and exploited other peoples, and destroyed their cultures. Western nations demanded for themselves a kind of Christianity that was mixed with the mission to conquer the world. Based on racial considerations, Western Christianity was declared superior. The geographically and personally determined names of some churches (e.g. Church of England, Church of Scotland, Dutch Reformed Church, Roman Catholic Church, Lutheran Church) are reminiscent of a nationalistic or particularistic colour of the Chris-

---

[82] Cf. Steven Paas, *Liefde voor Israël nader bekeken: Voor het Evangelie zijn alle volken gelijk,* Kampen: Brevier, 2015.

tian faith and mission. In the conquered territories, the Western mother church was placed above the indigenous churches. In countries like South Africa, this led to systems of apartheid, which even forbade the communion of holy supper and marriage between Christians of different ethnic origins.

Western Christianity allowed itself to be used for supporting the economic and political advantages of colonial powers. Today, this attitude still resonates when Christians from their privileged countries call 'Own people first' or 'We defend Fortress Europe' to the world struggling with problems of war, poverty and hunger. This practice has seriously damaged the credibility of the Christian faith for many vulnerable people. That is why the missionary capacity of Western Christians and congregations has been weakened or paralyzed.

To the harmful connection between a supposedly superior Christianity and the selfish demands of particular geographical areas and nations another aspect was added after the second world war. It concerns the position of Israel and the Jewish people in the consciousness of guilt in Western cultures. Apparently, opinions about the relationship between the church and Israel are closely linked to visions of the missionary character of the congregation.

In chapter 2, section c, we saw that according to certain Christians the church has taken the place of the Old Testament Israel, as a specifically divinely elected ethnic people. Other Christians (often vehemently) oppose this vision because they think God's election of the people of Old Testament Israel has continued after Calvary. In their view, Israel – apart from the church – is still God's unique people having a separate status on the way to salvation. They stress that the congregation must realize that she is of Jewish origin and act accordingly.

In my opinion both visions are unbiblical. The first view is ruled by the theory of replacement, debasing Israel, the second by the desire to unduly elevate the status of contemporary Israel or to 'judaize' the congregation. Although they differ from each other and oppose each other, both impose on the church Old Testament rules and structures. They fail to (fully) acknowledge that these Old Testament realities have received a different and deeper meaning in Christ, which transcends and goes beyond an image of the congregation that is determined by ethnic Israel. Such an image goes against the work of Christ and the apostles. In his account of Paul's missionary activities in Galatia, Gene Edwards paraphrases the apostle as follows: 'We have been called and sent to the gentiles, but not to put those gentiles in a Jewish culture afterwards'.[83] Although many Christians do not recognize themselves in these two extreme Israel visions, they are in their spheres of influence. Their faith may be mixed with the idea that some Israel vision is decisive to it. However, the most important question is not, 'What do you think of Israel?', but 'What do you think of the Christ?'

e. Divisions

What attracts people to obeying the great commission of Jesus? In the final analysis, it is just the attractiveness of the Sender Himself. Anyone who reads the Gospels must be impressed by His words and deeds, as a human being. For Christians, this noble Person is God's Son and their Saviour. Therefore, strikingly, it is precisely the apparent disobedience of Christians to a deep desire of Jesus for unity, which have made Him and His mission unattractive in the perception of many in the world and the church.

In His statements after the Last Supper and prior to His capture, Jesus admonished His disciples – and therefore all Christians and the church of all times and places – to preserve unity. He referred to a unity rooted in the love of God. The unbreakable and loving unity of the relationship between the Father and the Son should be the very characteristic of the unity between the followers of Jesus. This is how He addressed His Father in prayer:

---

[83] Gene Edwards, *De memoires van Silas: Een ongelooflijk avontuur dat de wereld veranderde*. Gideon 2011, p.206. The book retells the missionary activities of Paul in establishing congregations in Galatia and his struggle to win them back after a coup by judaizing preachers.

> 'Holy Father, protect them by the power of Your name – the name You gave Me – so that they may be one as We are one' (John17:11).

All Christians are challenged to respond to the requirement of unity based on the love of God. This is apparent from the dual commandment of love given by Jesus.[84] All commandments, indeed the whole of Scripture, depend on this instruction to love. Subsequently, it appears from the words of Jesus that the love of His followers for God and each other is of fundamental significance for participation in the great commission:

> 'A new command I give you: Love one another. As I have loved you, so you must love one another. By this all men will know that you are My disciples, if you love one another' (John 13:34,35).

Probably no teaching by Jesus has been disobeyed more seriously than the command to His followers to keep unity and love. For authentic witness in the world, the credibility of the gospel depends on the loving unity of the Christians who are spreading the joyful message. The disrupted unity of the congregation (church), torn apart in numerous groups, is a public disgrace. As a result, the carrying out of the great commission of Jesus has been seriously crippled. The world is confused about Jesus' message from so many mouths, often opposing each other vehemently. Many do not recognize Him in His messengers. Is it any wonder that in the West the masses have turned away from Him?[85]

f. Introversion

By this term I mean the phenomenon of being focussed inwardly. Not as a mental illness of individuals, or of a person being reticent or taciturn by character, but as a theological or spiritual

---

[84] Cf. chapter 3, section b.

[85] A sad symbol of divided Christianity is the Church of the Holy Sepulchre in Jerusalem, divided into sections among several denominations who have often come to blows with each other like children in a playground. A Muslim keeps stewardship over the facility and acts as a referee among the Christians because they act so shamefully in their competition with each other.

mode of existence of congregations, and consequently of their members. Among them a lot of attention is paid to the individual perspective, personal salvation, or to a specific internal structure of the congregation, which reflects this. Introversion also characterizes the preaching and the pastoral care. The need for self-reflection is stressed: 'Am I converted?' Of course, as such there is nothing wrong with that question. Asking it is good and even necessary. Undoubtedly, the church is meant to be a body that is called and equipped to lead persons to Jesus for receiving personal salvation. It is a matter of course to encourage self-examination, and consider one's status in the faith based on his or her relationship with Jesus. As such, this does not create a climate of spiritual individualism or selfishness.

However, this is different from when this inward focus one-sidedly controls the structure of the congregation and her spirituality. The condition of personal salvation can be so over-emphasized to the neglect of other vital issues that the confession of the church as the 'communion of saints' becomes an empty slogan. If the congregation becomes so lopsided in its emphasis its very survival will eventually be in danger. Why would you be a member of the congregation if you don't have any meaningful relationship with anyone?

Moreover, in a setting of introversion the importance of the task to lead people outside the municipality to Christ and salvation becomes less urgent. Increasingly, among the members that missionary impulse can gradually fade and eventually vanish. The natural external focus of the congregation as an organism for participating in Jesus' great commission is in danger of getting lost. This is a serious matter, because it touches the essential identity of the congregation as a building of Christ (Hebr.3:6).

This dangerous process of introversion can be recognized by looking at its characteristics of 'enlargement' and 'reduction'. Internal characteristics of the congregation are enlarged or magnified and outward-looking aspects are reduced or made insignificant. Forms of 'enlargement' in congregations that focus inwardly appear when all kinds of details of the organisational structure of the congregation, of the doctrine, and of the personal faith of the members are increasingly determined in minute details, which are then considered to be of final importance. This shows that the character of the congregation has shifted. The spiritual perspectives, including missionary motivation, have narrowed down in importance. Preservation of the own inward characteristics have become the first goal and the criterion for the assessing the outside world.

Often, such congregations tend to profile themselves regarding congregations that put different accents. This is one of the main causes of ecclesiastical divisions (see section e. above). In introverted congregations members sometimes tend to avoid the meetings. They do not really feel the need for being in connection or communion with fellow believers. In their tendency to spiritual individualism they undervalue the effect of meeting with other Christians. Initially, perhaps the services are still 'attended' via the Internet, but gradually the involvement with the community of the congregation decreases. In summary, it can be said that introverted congregations have less regard for their missionary task in the world. The consciousness that the church of Jesus exists for the purpose of being a missionary communion has weakened. Ultimately, this endangers the very existence of the congregation.

The great commission of Jesus does not define the congregation as a closed organization, but as an open missionary organism. Her outward-looking mission, the spread of the gospel, should be supported by all her internal characteristics: those of the faith of the Christians, the sections of the organization, the content of preaching, the pastoral care, and the diaconate.

g. Adjustment problems

The congregation has to make herself as accessible as possible to outsiders. That requires certain forms of adjustment. Jesus has preceded us in this course of action. After all, in His coming to the world, the Son of God utterly adapted Himself to us. By becoming human, He made himself accessible to us. In the most literal sense He has become 'flesh'. That is why we call this the *incarnation* of Christ. We also call it the *condescendence* of God: He has bowed down to us in Christ. Jesus has come to be next to us, within our reach, to be understood, felt and believed. Jesus expects congregations and individual Christians to follow His example. In other words, we need to make ourselves accessible. That requires taking initiatives, in order to become familiar with the language, living conditions, and the culture of outsiders. That goes beyond just the acquisition of intellectual knowledge, we also need to adapt as much as possible to their speech, living conditions and culture. This requires meeting people 'where they are'.

The need for adaptation is most apparent when we are approaching people of non-Western background. Then, it may be necessary to learn a foreign language and to acquaint oneself with a foreign culture. We must realize that all languages – not just our Western languages (!) – show something of the beauty of God's creation.[86] The fact that mission includes language learning and making translations has been known since the Greek version of the Old Testament, the *Septuagint*, emerged in the third century BC.[87] Since then, the language aspect of mission has remained important; ultimately it has developed into a separate branch of missionary science.[88]

Adaptation is linked to the need to recognize, acknowledge and use points of contact with the adherents of other religions and cultures, far away in other continents, and

---

[86] Steven Paas, 'Your language is God's creation': Speech at the launch of our *Oxford Chichewa Dictionary*, Lilongwe, September 2016.

[87] G. van 't Wout, *De receptie van het Oude Testament in de Wereldzending*, Universiteit van Utrecht, 1989, describes translations of the Old Testament and their spreading from Antiquity 1960.

[88] J.A.B. Jongeneel, *Missiologie, deel I 'Zendingswetenschap'*, Den Haag: Boekencentrum, 1986, p.122-131, introduction to missionary linguistics. Haak, *Gereformeerde Missiologie & Oecumene*, p.144: introduction to cross- and intercultural communication and linguistics. Thorsten Prill, 'The use of English in cross-cultural mission: observations from Africa', unpublished essay, 2020.

nearby in our own multi-cultural society. If we have little or no understanding for this necessity, this may be the result of the influences of Western superiority thinking that we have discussed before.[89] Unwittingly, cultural arrogance can have got in the way of mission.

We recommend to all Christians to assist in the work of teaching strangers our own language and culture. As a result, spontaneously good contacts may be established with fellow human beings from other cultures and religions, thus creating for them an access to the gospel. But also within our Western culture, great differences have grown between people. The climate in the congregation and among Christians has become almost unrecognisable to the surrounding secular culture. Sometimes, we seem to have come from different planets. In order to land the gospel, it is necessary that Christians understand the environment and the worldviews of their 'neighbours', who are completely alien to the Christian faith.

Finally, adaptation or adjustment undoubtedly concerns the way in which the Word of God is communicated. Western people and people of other cultures often have different antennas.[90] People who grew up with the Bible differ in mindset from people for whom the Bible is a strange book. Our approaches and methods fail if we do not tune them to the frequency of the recipients. In missiological terminology, this regards the need for *contextualisation*.[91]

Most of the discussed hindrances weaken the willingness to adapt. This is particularly true for the congregations where there is a spirit of division, inequality, racial or cultural apartheid, and introversion It is important to address those problems.

---

[89] See chapter 2, section d; chapter 4, sections c, d, en e.

[90] Thorsten Prill, 'Church Culture, Gospel Proclamation and Superiority', 2020.

[91] Cf. chapter 4, section d; chapter 6, section b.

10. Be strong in weakness

a. Understanding

Numerous Christians have obeyed the great commission of Jesus. They became participants in His mission to draw the Kingdom of God nearer. We can read about their work and its effect in a large number of publications about mission history. Some accessible introductory books are recommended here.[92] In addition, I refer to some extensive recent sources of a scholarly character.[93]

As a result of the mission activities in many countries on all continents the phenomenon of Christianity and representations of the congregation/church have taken shape. Publications on church history testify to this.[94] The existence of separate books on church history and on the history of mission history indicates that mission has often been considered as a task of specialized members of the congregation. The obvious truth that essentially *all* Christians are missionaries in their own context has remained underrepresented.

The idea as such that not every Christian is suitable to participate in the mission of Jesus is not surprising. After all, we can be intimidated by the extensive task, the commitment demanded, or the often risky beginning in our own environment. That is why we can understand the many excuses and obstacles that Christians and their congregations have taken into account when confronted with the urgent appeal of Jesus.

---

[92] For useful brief surveys, see e.g.: Robert, Dana L., *Christian Mission: How Christianity Became a World Religion*, Wiley- Blackwell, 2009; Timothy Nyasulu, *Missiology: A Study of the Spread of the Christian Faith*, Kachere Tools No 2, Zomba, 2004.

[93] Here are two examples of recent scholarly works of the history of mission: Dale T. Irvin en Scott W. Sunquist, *History of the World Christian Movement*, 3 vols, Edinburgh: T&T Clark, 2001-2012. Klaus Wetzel, *Die Geschichte der christlichen Mission: Von der Antike bis zur Gegenwart – Ein Kompendium*, Gießen: Brunnen Verlag, 2019. Other useful scholarly sources are in the bibliography.

[94] See for example the detailed bibliographies in my: *Christianity in Eurafrica*.

However, our understanding the problem does not solve the problem.

b. Recognizing weakness

What is the solution to this problem? How can *all* Christians at *all* segments of the congregation, as an institute and as an organism, with *all* aspects of their existence get engaged in the spread of the gospel in the world? This is possible, first of all, by recognising in the light of the Sender that not any Christian is capable of doing so in his or her own strength. Jesus, who sends us, is also the One who gives us the power and the ability to do so.

Essentially, He Himself is the performer of the missionary task. After all, He has been sent, as the Son of God. We must always realize that mission is entirely the work of God. In Christ, He is in the process of advancing His Kingdom. The signs of His approaching Kingdom He is showing here and now. For this work He wants to engage all Christians and all congregations. Because of this reality our mission activities are different from simply obeying an order or command. Having a missionary attitude is about becoming sensitive and dependent on the Spirit, in order to see where God calls us and where He is at work. Perceiving the signs of His presence, we join Him in testimony and service. With His Christ, the Sent One, God works through the brothers and sisters of Christ. Christians participate in the mission of Jesus, as members of His Body. They are 100 percent dependent on Him. They do not want to hinder Him when He forms His congregation, but as children of God they are instruments in His hands (2 Tim.2:21), partakers in His work.[95]

While realising that Christ has sent them, Christians do not pretend being braver or better than they are. They have discovered that their obedience to the great commission is anything but perfect. Like the disciples who were first in receiving

---

[95] Edwards, *The Silas Diary*, concludes that if you leave a congregation to Christ, you may be assured that His Body, the people of God, will find ways to maintain itself.

Jesus' missional words, they are sometimes attacked by doubts (Mt.28:17). To their grief, they experience that they are still weak in faith and knowledge and that sin still plays a role in their lives. However, they do not rest in that experience, but they flee with their weakness to Jesus. It appears that the power of Jesus is accomplished in their weakness. Paul knew that: 'For when I am weak, then I am strong' (2 Cor.12:10).

The power of Christ overcomes the weakness in the lives of the believers. That is why, as Christians and as a congregation, we are not sent into the world in our own strength, but in the power of Jesus.

c. Grace and Love

We can only do the work of Jesus Christ through the grace of the tri-une God, who came to us in the Son. We live and work through His grace. This is evident from the blessing with which God greets us, for example at the end of a church meeting, when we are ready again to go into the world of our daily life.

> 'May the grace of the Lord Jesus Christ, and the love of God, and the fellowship of the Holy Spirit be with you all' (2 Cor.13:13).

That powerful blessing and greeting from God prepares Christians for the next steps on the mission road. In this divine blessing, the Son reaches out to us first, with His grace. Then follows the Father with His love for us, and the Spirit, who binds us together with Him and with each other. That order should not be taken for granted.

God's love is the cause and the origin of the great commission.[96] But the wonderful love of God can only be understood to a certain extent when we realize that He loves us because He is merciful in Christ. In fact, God expresses His love in Christ. In a sense, Christ is the love of God. God's love is inseparably connected to the incomprehensibly great grace of Christ toward us. It is precisely because of this grace and love that it is possible for Christians to function in the world as participants in the *Missio Dei*, God's mission. For that matter, the

---

[96] See: chapter 1, section a; chapter 3, section b3.

love of God and the grace of Christ liberate us from the worst hindrance to mission there is: our natural rebellion against God because of sin. Our sinful nature – with a crippling weakness in its wake – deserves the punishment of eternal death. But on the cross, Christ has taken over our guilt and has removed the punishment of condemnation. He redeemed us for service in His Kingdom. That grants us the love and the grateful willingness to participate in carrying out the great commission of the Sent One, who also is our Sender. We want nothing more than to testify to our Lord, in words and deeds, because we love Him.[97]

d. Through the Holy Spirit

But how does this work in practice? The grace of God the Son and the all-embracing love of God the Father is to function in the concrete relationship between (Western) Christians and their neighbours. Most people in the congregation are afraid of sharing the faith with their neighbours. They realize that Jesus' great commission has been given to them too, but they compare their own smallness and limitations to the impressive power and influence of the opposing elements in the culture in which they live.

However, they are not alone. Paul says that the love of God has been poured into the hearts of Christians by the Holy Spirit (Rom.5:5). Chapter 1 already showed that mission is a trinitarian matter, a mission of the tri-une God. The power of the Holy Spirit, through which Christians have become reborn children of God, remains available to them.

The Holy Spirit has been sent by the Father and the Son. He is the great Performer by Whom the Father and the Son work in their *Missio Dei* in the world. When God sends His Son, and when the Son sends His disciples, it is the Holy Spirit who puts this into practice. He is the source of power for those who participate in the great commission. If we were to rely

---

[97] W. van Heest, 'Woord en daad in het Nieuwe Testament', in: Joosse (red.), *Zending dichterbij*, deel I, 1992, p.25-61: Mission is a matter of love of neighbour, expressing itself in the agreement between words and deeds (p.57). Van Heest was a missionary on the Indonesian island Sulawesi.

solely on our own piety, intelligence and capabilities, our efforts would be too weak. After all, since the Old Testament the Almighty Lord has made no the participants in His great commission: 'Not by might nor by power, but by My Spirit' it will happen (Zech 4:6).In addition to the missional words of Jesus, Christians always need the Holy Spirit. This truth affects all the topics that have been raised in this booklet.

Through the Spirit, we realize that missionary work begins with our neighbours, but does not end there. The Spirit makes us sensitive to the common ground or points of contact between the faith we received from God and the beauty that God has left in people who do not (want to) know Him. The Spirit delivers us from the self-image of superiority that we as Christians in Western culture – often unwittingly – show in our communication with refugees or migrants from other cultures. The Spirit makes us understand the christocentric character of the entire Bible and thus the fulfilment in Christ of the position of Old Testament Israel and the Jews. The Spirit strengthens our missionary consciousness by giving confidence in the unlimited scope of Christ's work, including the shedding of His atoning blood on the cross at Calvary. The Holy Spirit overcomes evasive attitudes and barriers or hindrances among Christians, which have weakened or paralyzed mission in the West. Through the work of the Holy Spirit, the great commission of Jesus to participate in His work continues to address the hearts and the heads of all Christians of all times and places. As a result, by definition the congregation (the church) is a missionary organism of the Holy Spirit, which has profound consequences for its organization as an institution and for the spiritual attitude of its members.

Now that such a powerful Ally is on our side, we can participate in the *Missio Dei* of the Father and the Son, because the Spirit has given us a new life, together with His missionary power. Therefore, as a Christian community and as members of Jesus Christ, let us try to find the hearts and heads of our neighbours, who do not yet know His wondrous grace and love.

Bibliography

Anderson, Gerald H.(Ed.), *Biographical Dictionary of Christian Missions*, Grand Rapids: Eerdmans, 1959.

Augustiny, Waldemar, *Ga heen en verkondig: Twintig eeuwen christelijke zending*, vert. H.A. Wiersinga, Wageningen: Zomer & Keunings, 1963.

Bauckham, Richard, *The Bible and Mission: Christian Witness in a Postmodern World*, Baker Publ., 2004.

Boer, C.P. de, *Christos Sunthronos: Een onderzoek naar de herkomst en het karakter van verwijzingen naar LXX Ps 109 in het Nieuwe Testament*, dissertatie TUA, januari 2020.

Bosch, David J., *Transforming Mission: Paradigm Shifts in Theology of Mission*, New York: Maryknoll, 1993 (eerst 1991).

Breman, Christina Maria, *The Associaton of Evangelicals in Africa: Its History, Organization, Members, Projects, External Relations and Message*, Zoetermeer: Boekencentrum, 1996

Bruijn, Steef de, 'Oudjaar voor apatheïsten', *RD Magazine*, 28-12-19, p.17.

Calvin, John, John Calvin, *Institutes of the Christian Religion* [transl. Henry Beveridge], Grand Rapids: Eerdmans, 1989.

Canons of Dort, https://www.apuritansmind.com/creeds-and-confessions/the-synod-of-dordt-1618-1619-a-d/

Carlier, J.H. e.a. (red.), *Uw Koninkrijk kome – Terugziend naar het verleden, actief in het heden: 60 jaar zending van de Christ. Geref. Kerken*, Hilversum, 1989.

CGK, Studierapport van deputaten Kerk en Israël van de christelijke gereformeerde kerken, "Wat betekent de term 'Israël' in kerk en theologie?", uitgebracht aan de CGK Synode van december 2019 [36 pagina's A4]. www.kerkenisrael.nl/studie

Coleman, M. en P Verster, 'Contextualisation of the Gospel among Muslims', in: *Acta Theologica*, 2006-2, p. 94-115. file:///C:/Users/Gebruiker/Downloads/49037-65096-1-PB.pdf

Cragg, Kenneth, *The Call of the Minaret*, New York: Orbis Books/ Maryknoll and Ibadan: Daystar Press, 1985[3].

Dalrymple, Rob, *These Brothers of Mine: A Biblical Theology of Land and Family and a Response to Christian Zionism*, Eugene, Oregon: Wipf & Stock, 2015. http://www.determinetruth.com/about-me.html

De Jong, Gerald F., *The Dutch Reformed Church and Negro Slavery in Colonial America*, reprint from *Church History*, 1971, vol. xxx, No.4.

Edwards, Gene, *The Silas Diary: The Story of an Incredible Adventure that Changed the World*, SeedSowers, 2005.

Challenging Western Christians and their Neighbours

Flemming, Dean, *Contextualization in the New Testament: Patterns for Theology and Mission*, Intervarsity, 2005.

Frend, W.C.H., *The Donatist Church: A Movement of Protest in Roman Northern Africa*, Oxford University Press, 1985[2]

Goheen, Micheal W., *A Light to the Nations: The Missional Church and the Biblical Story*, Baker Academic, 2011.

Haak, C.J., *Gereformeerde Missiologie en Oecumenica: Beknopt overzicht aan het begin van de 21ste eeuw A.D.*, Zwolle: De Verre Naasten, 2005.

Hammond, Peter, *The Greatest Century of Missions*, Howard Place: Christian Liberty Books, 1982.

Harrison, Peter, *The Territories of Science and Religion*, University of Chicago, 2017 (first 2015).

Hill, Jonathan, *Christianity, the First 400 Years*, Lion Hudson, 2013.

Hof, I.P.C. van 't, *Het zendingsbegrip van Karl Bart*, Hoenderloo: Zendingsstudieraad, 1946.

Holland, Tom, *Dominion: The making of the Western Mind*, Little Rock UK, January 2019.

Irvin, Dale T. en Scott W. Sunquist, *History of the World Christian Movement*, 3 vols, Edinburgh: T&T Clark, 2012.

Jabini, Franklin Steven, *Christianity in Suriname: An Overview of its History, Theologians and Sources*, Carlisle: Langham, 2012.

Jansen, J.G.B. (Hans), *Christelijke theologie na Auschwitz*, deel 3: *De geschiedenis van 2000 jaar kerkelijk antisemitisme*, Amsterdam: Blaak, 1999.

Jongeneel, J.A.B., *Missiologie, deel I, 'Zendingswetenschap'*, Den Haag: Boekencentrum, 1986.

Joosse, L.J., e.a. (red.), *Zending Dichterbij*, deel I: 'Leren hoe hij wand'len moet – over woord en daad in de zending', Goes: Oosterbaan & Le Cointre, 1992.

Kane, J. Herbert, *A Concise History of the Christian World Mission*, Baker, 1982.

Kato, Byang H, *Theological Pitfalls in Africa*, University of Virginia: Evangelical Publ. House, 1975.

Kommers, J (Hans), *En zij volgen het lichtend spoor: Kleine geschiedenis van de zending* [226 pagina's], Artiosreeks, Heerenveen: Groen, 2019.

Kroesbergen, Hermen, *The Language of Faith in Southern Africa: Spirit World, Power, Community, Holism*, Cape Town: AOSIS, 2019.

Maljaars, Bram, *Het Getuigenis van Jezus: De sleutel tot het verstaan van de profetieën*, Soest: Boekscout, 2018.

———, 'And so All Israel will be saved (Rom.11:26)', in: Paas, *Christian Zionism Examined*, Appendix I.

McLeod, Cynthia, *The cost of the Sugar,* London: HopeRoad, 2013 (first, 1987).

McDonald, Thomas Michael, *The Black Book: Native Americans and the Christian Experience – Overcoming the Negative Impact of Nominal Christianity*, Manitoba, Canada: Goldrock Press, 2017 (first, 2004).

McGrath, Alister E., 'Natural Theology? The Barth–Brunner Debate of 1934' [http://onlinelibrary.wiley.com/doi/10.1002/9781118569276.ch4/summary].

Meyer, Birgit, '*Christianity in Africa: From African Independent to Pentecostal-Charismatic Churches*', in: *Annual Review of Anthropology,* Vol. 33 (2004), p. 447-474.

Msiska, Stephen Kauta, *Golden Buttons: Christianity and Traditional Religion among the Tumbuka*, Blantyre: Christian Literature Association of Malawi, 1997.

Mwanza, Chopo, 'To Western Missionaries: From an African Pastor' [https://africa.thegospelcoalition.org/article/western-missionaries-african-pastor/].

Ngwena, Charles, *What is Africanness?: Contesting nativism in race, culture and sexualities*, Pretoria University Law Press, 2018.

Newbigin, Lesslie, *The Gospel in a Pluralist Society*, Eerdmans, 1989, p.13 - 36.

Noortwijk, Floor van, 'Canada's gebroken mozaiek: Een multiculturele natie verwikkeld in een verleden vol mythes?', BA-thesis, University of Utrecht, 2019.

Nyasulu, Timothy, *Missiology: A Study of the Spread of the Christian Faith*, Kachere Tools No 2, Zomba, 2004.

Paas, Stefan, *Pilgrims and Priests: Christian Mission in a Post-Christian Society*, London: SCM Press, 2019.

———, *Church Planting in the Secular West: Learning from the European Experience*, Grand Rapids: Eerdmans, 2016.

Paas, Steven,, *A Conflict on Authority in the Early African Church: Augustine of Hippo and the Donatists*, Zomba: Kachere, 2005.

———, *Israëlvisies in beweging: Gevolgen voor kerk, geloof en theologie*, Kampen: Brevier 2014.

———, *Liefde voor Israël nader bekeken: Voor het Evangelie zijn alle volken gelijk,* Kampen: Brevier, 2015.

———, *Oxford Chichewa Dictionary*, Cape Town: Oxford University Press [Orbis], 2016. https://translate.chichewadictionary.org/

———, 'Your language is God's creation': Speech at the launch of the Oxford Chichewa Dictionary, Lilongwe, September 2016. http://chichewadictionary.org/media/speech_Launch_Oxford_Chichewa_Dictionary-LLW_29-9-16.pdf

———, *Christianity in Eurafrica: A History of the Church in Europe and Africa*, Washington DC: New Academia Publishing, 2017.

103

————, (Ed.), *Israelism and the Place of Christ: Christocentric Interpretation of Biblical Prophecy*, LIT Verlag, Berlin, Munster,Vienna, Zurich, London, January 2018.

————, *Luther on Jews and Judaism: A Review of his 'Judenschriften'*, Zürich: LIT Verlag, 2017.

————, *Johannes Rebmann: A Servant of God in Africa Before the Rise of Western Colonialism*, Bonn: Verlag für Kultur und Wissenschaft, 2018.

————, Review of: Apawo en Werner, *Anthology of African Christianity*, in: *The Ecumenical Review*, WCC, November 2019, p.245-248.

————, *Christian Zionism Examined: A Review of Ideas on Israel, the Church, and the Kingdom*. Second edition, Eugene, Oregon: Wipf & Stock, 2020.

Phiri, Isabel Apawo en Dietrich Werner (chief editors), *Anthology of African Christianity*, Oxford: Regnum Books, 2016.

Prill, Thorsten, 'Church Culture, Gospel Proclamation and Superiority', un-published essay, Namibia Evangelical Theological Seminary/ Edinburgh Bible College, 2020.

————, 'The use of English in cross-cultural mission: observations from Africa', unpublished essay, Namibia Evangelical Theological Seminary/ Edinburgh Bible College, 2020.

Richardson, Don, 'A World Prepared for the Gospel: The Melchizedek Factor', in: *Eternity in Their Hearts*, Minneapolis: Bethany House, 2014 (first,1981), p.9-136.

Robert, Dana L., *Christian Mission: How Christianity Became a World Religion*, Wiley- Blackwell, 2009.

Sanders, E., 'A Theological Study of Point of Contact Theory', in: *Global Missiology*, Contemporary Practice, July 2004
[http://ojs.globalmissiology.org/index.php/english/article/viewFile/109/313]

Senior, Donald & Carroll Stuhlmueller, *The Biblical Foundations for Mission*, London: SCM Press, 1984.

Thomson, Peter J., 'Harnack, Marcion: das Evangelium vom fremden Gott'
[file:///C:/Users/Gebruiker/Downloads/Harnack%20Marcion%20NTT%2067%20(2013)%2056-64%20(1).pdf]

Turaki, Yusufu, *Foundations of African Traditional Religion and Worldview*, Nairobi: Word Alive, 2006.

Twiss, Richard, *Rescuing the Gospel from the Cowboys: A Native American Expression of the Jesus Way*, Downers Grove: Inter Varsity Press 2015 (earlier, 1996, 2004, 2007).

Verkuijl, J., *Breek de muren af!: Om gerechtigheid in de rassenverhoudingen*, Baarn: Bos & Keuning, 1971.

————, *Contemporary Missiology: An Introduction*, Grand Rapids: Eerdmans, 1978.

Wetzel, Klaus, *Die Geschichte der christlichen Mission: Von der Antike bis zur Gegenwart – Ein Kompendium*, Gießen: Brunnen Verlag, 2019.

White, E. Blake, *God's Chosen People: Promised to Israel – Fulfilled in the Church*, Colorado Springs: Cross to Crown Ministries, 2017.

Wind, A., *Zending en Oecumene in de twintigste eeuw*, deel I, 'Van Edinburgh 1910 tot en met Evanston 1954'. Kampen: Kok, 1984.

Wout, G. van 't, *De receptie van het Oude Testament in de Wereldzending*, doctoraalscriptie Universiteit van Utrecht, 1989.

Wright, Christopher J.H., *The Mission of God: Unlocking the Bible's Grand Narrative*, InterVarsity, 2013.

Wyngaard, George Jacobus (Cobus) van, *In Search of Repair: Critical white responses to whiteness as a theological problem – a South African contribution*, doctoral thesis, Vrije Universiteit, Amsterdam, December 2019.

Yates, Timothy, *Christian Mission in the Twentieth Century*, Cambridge University, 1996.

Ziel, Kees van der, *Kom uit je wigwam: in de kraamkamer van een bijbelvertaalproject bij de Karaïben*, Barnabas, 2000.

———, 'Door het oog van de naald. Cultuur, context en bijbelvertaling bij de Karaïben', in: *Wereld en Zending. Tijdschrift voor Interculturele theologie*. Jrg. 31, 2003, p. 47-60.

The same Author

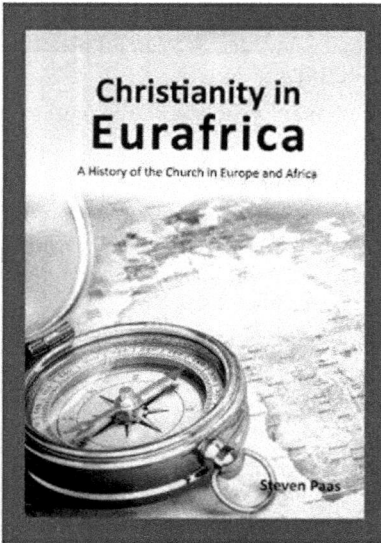

Christianity in Eurafrica: A History of the Church in Europe and Africa, Washington DC: *New Academia Publishing* (NAP), February 2017/ Wellington (South Africa), by *Christian Literature Fund* (CLF), March 2016.

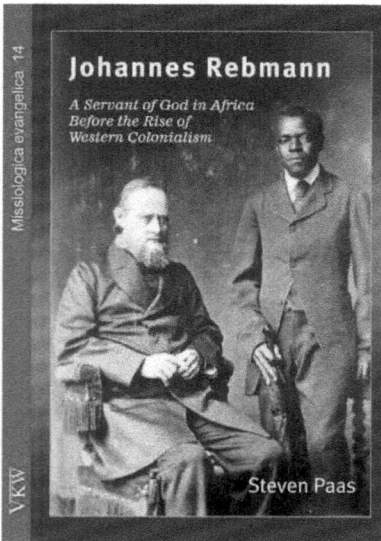

Johannes Rebmann: A Servant of God in Africa Before the Rise of Western Colonialism, second edition (updated, enlarged), Bonn: Verlag für Kultur und Wissenschaft (VKW)/ Eugene, Oregon (USA): Wipf & Stock, May 2018 [First ed. Nürnberg: VTR, 2011]

www.ingramcontent.com/pod-product-compliance
Lightning Source LLC
Chambersburg PA
CBHW060418090426
42734CB00011B/2360